The Great Utopian Delusion

By Clarence B. Carson

The Fateful Turn
The American Tradition
The Flight from Reality
The War on the Poor
Throttling the Railroads
The Rebirth of Liberty
The World in the Grip of an Idea
Organized Against Whom?
    The Labor Union in America
The Colonial Experience
The Beginning of the Republic
The Sections and the Civil War
The Growth of America
The Welfare State
America in Gridlock
A Teacher's Guide to A Basic History of the U.S.
Basic Economics
Basic Communism
Basic American Government
Swimming Against the Tide

By Clarence B. Carson and Paul A. Cleveland

Basic Economics, 3rd edition

By Paul A. Cleveland

Understanding the Modern Culture Wars
Unmasking the Sacred Lies

By Brian McGrath and L. Dwayne Barney

Capital as Money

The Great Utopian Delusion

The Global Rise of Government and
the Destruction of Liberty

Clarence B. Carson

Paul A. Cleveland

L. Dwayne Barney

Boundary Stone • Birmingham, Alabama

© 2015 Paul A. Cleveland
All rights reserved.
First Printing
Printed in The United States of America

No part of this publication may be reproduced, stored in a retrieval system, or transmitted in any form by any means, electronic, mechanical, photocopy, recording, or otherwise, without prior written permission of Boundary Stone LLC, except for brief quotations in critical reviews or articles.

Scripture taken from the NEW AMERICAN STANDARD BIBLE®, ©1960,1962,1963,1968,1971,1972,1973,1975,1977,1995 by The Lockman Foundation. Used by permission.

ISBN: 978-0-9727401-3-5
Library of Congress Control Number: 2015937581

Dust jacket design: Dwayne Cogdill, Saint Dwayne Design
Cover photo: ingimage
Index: Ina Gravitz

Boundary Stone
P.O. Box 19515
Birmingham, AL 35219
www.boundarystone.org

This book is dedicated to R. Nelson Nash.

Contents

Preface	ix
The Idea That Has the World in Its Grip	1
Revolutionary vs. Evolutionary Socialism	15
The Need to Deceive	29
The Massive State and the Impotent Populace	41
Coercing Our Way to Paradise	53
People Confused and Abused by Rules Gone Wild	69
The Real Victim	81
Embracing Responsibility	93
Acknowledgements	103
Notes	105
Index	107

PREFACE

The lead author and the subject matter of this book need some explanation. In the 1970s, a mentor of mine, Dr. Clarence Carson wrote a series of articles for *The Freeman* that was eventually published as a book titled, *The World in the Grip of an Idea*. Put most simply, he argued that the idea that has the world in its grip is utopianism. While few would claim to be utopian in their thinking, the prevailing belief that governmental means can be used to remedy any and all human ills that we face proves otherwise.

Dr. Carson was a historian by training. But he also possessed an uncanny ability to peer into the depths of political economy to clearly explain the circumstances of society. This brought a deeper level of understanding to those of us fortunate enough to learn from him directly and from his many books and other writings.

Dr. Carson passed away in 2003 so it might seem odd that his name appears as the lead author on this new book. Nevertheless, that placement is well deserved. Last year a mutual friend of Dr. Carson and myself came to me and suggested that the original book needed to be republished. However, that book is quite long and academic. In addition, much has happened in the nearly forty years since the original publication. One important event was the collapse of the former Soviet Union. Despite these factors there are many important ideas in the original book that are as relevant today as they were when it was written. Indeed, the main idea is perhaps more relevant today as the nations of the world seem headstrong in their efforts to plunge toward socialism. If not reversed, the end result of this movement will be hardship and suffering and, in the end, economic collapse as was experienced in the former Soviet empire. Dr. Carson's keen insight into the underlying reason for the spread of socialism in the 70s can clearly be applied today.

It is with this in mind that Dwayne Barney and I set out to mine the original book for its gold, so to speak, and to present it in a manner that anyone can read and understand. Furthermore, we've updated the material where it was needed in order to make the case for today's audience. Our hope in doing so is that our readers will understand the perils of listening to socialist reformers and reject their poisonous elixir of political economy.

Paul A. Cleveland

One

The Idea That Has the World in Its Grip

Do you long for a better world? Would you like to see the many wrongs around you set right? Do you wish that everyone lived in a world of peace and justice? No doubt, everyone would answer yes to these questions. At times we have all suffered in this life. It might have been the abuse we took at work with an ungrateful and harsh employer. We have probably all felt cheated at some point by a company we thought failed to keep its end of the bargain. Or, we have all purchased something we discovered we really did not want only to find that the store would not allow us to return it. Then, too, we all have been violated by other people in our countless interpersonal relationships. These violations leave us feeling alienated from others and even from ourselves.

As we long for a better world many are tempted by the siren song of socialism. The various failings and ills of life in this world are obvious. This is why the lure seems so strong. Proponents of socialism tell us that if government power can only be directed in the correct way, all that plagues us will disappear. In fact, Karl Marx promised that all alienation would vanish once communism replaced capitalism. But, is that promise a lie? Could it be that succumbing to the temptation will result in the very opposite of that which was promised? Could it be that embracing socialism will result in greater abuse, hardship, and suffering in this world? We believe that the answer to these questions is yes.

The short answer as to why this is true is that it is vanity to think that we can obtain perfection in this world. Perfection cannot be obtained in a world that is comprised of very imperfect creatures. History books are littered with evidence that this is true. Since imperfect humans form all of our institutions, how can we expect there to ever be a perfect institution? No human effort can establish an institution that is perfect. While this is the short answer, much more needs to be said to make that case. In the pages that follow we aim to do just that and then to point out what action would actually lead to the true betterment of our neighbors and ourselves. While perfection cannot be achieved, embracing sound principles of human action can lead to a better situation.

Individual freedom has long been considered a hallmark characteristic of people living in America. The glaring exception of slavery, coupled with other notable areas of the failure to protect and promote the natural rights of life, liberty, and property were present after the nation's founding. Despite these exceptions, by and large people were remarkably free for the first century of America's existence. Most individuals were able to live out their lives according to their own plans and inclinations as long as they did not transgress the co-equal rights of others. The government did not intervene greatly in people's affairs. Freedom set Americans apart from the rest of the world. It made the country a desirable destination for everyone seeking the privileges of individual liberty and choice. It also spawned the desire in many to seek reforms in their own countries that might embrace individual freedom and liberty.

Even today, Americans are very vocal in describing their lives as free. If saying it is so made it so, individual freedom would be as much a characteristic of America today as when the country was originally founded. Sadly, that judgment cannot stand on its own merit. In truth the individual in the U.S. is restricted, regulated, taxed, hounded, harangued, and herded in all manner of ways. Government experts who "know better" what the individual really needs control virtually every decision from the basic choices of food, clothing, and shelter, to the choice of the kind of box in which to be buried.

Interestingly enough, despite all this coercion, most people still consider themselves to be free. It is reminiscent of a poster. The poster pictured a herd of sheep in a pasture with the caption reading, "Just because you can't see the fence doesn't mean you're free." There is a reason people do not see the reality of the intense limitations on their freedom. The reason for their blindness is that they have uncritically accepted an idea that cannot be true. Similar to an ever tightening vice, the grip of this idea continues to constrict the world in its grasp. The aim of this book is to explain the idea that has the world in its grip so as to allow the reader to recognize and counteract its effects.

From time to time phrases are concocted that say something that hardly needs to be said. These phrases are adopted because they frequently tell us something about what is new and different. Among many others, some contemporary examples are expressions such as "selfie" and "unfriend."

One phrase that came into currency sometime around World War II was "displaced person." "DPs," as they were called just after the war, could be seen wandering across Europe. They carried the remains of their pitiful possessions on their backs as they roamed here and there. They were Poles, Russians, Romanians, Latvians, and Ukrainians, forcefully moved away from their homes to work for the Germans during the war. Among the displaced persons were also Jews seeking some new homeland. After the war they were uncertain what to do or where to go. War had caused these people to be transplanted and the continuing revolution in Russia was just another factor completing their displacement.

"Displaced" is a strange word to use in connection with these people. The most common word formed from "displace" is "displacement." It is used to describe what happens, for example, when an object is placed in water. A certain volume of water is "displaced" when it is moved from where it was to a new location. It is usually a term for a mechanical operation. That is why it is unusual to use such a term to refer to people. People have wills; they may choose. Typically they are not something to be "displaced," as if they were water. Yet following World War II the phrase was descriptive. People were as near to being displaced as people are likely to be. They had been taken, held, and moved against their wills. The human forces that swept over them had displaced them.

Today the phrase is not used anymore. You are more likely to hear such people called "refugees." But refugees are, nonetheless, displaced persons. They have been displaced by revolutions and changes over which they had no control. They may have chosen to migrate, but they did not choose to lose their homes from which they had to flee. Men are as surely displaced by wars and revolutions as water is displaced when a ship is launched. This displacement and the efforts to avoid displacement are a major theme for our discussion here.

If the idea of displacement is to serve adequately for our purposes it must be expanded. There is both literal displacement and figurative displacement. In the figurative sense, it is possible to be displaced and yet never actually move from your original location. As an example of this, it was once commonplace that businesses reserved the right to deny service to anyone for any reason. Now, regulations and court decisions increasingly dictate to business owners who they must do business with. Failure to comply with such dictates can result in the loss of one's business altogether. While the business owner might not move out of his house, he has nevertheless been displaced. This kind of figurative displacement is widespread. It is not as dramatic as literal displacement, but it is just as real in its own way.

The sense of being at home means living in familiar surroundings; being in the right place. One's sense of being in the right place grows out of familiarity with the customs, the traditions, the mores, and the styles, and either being in accord with or having adjusted to them. The sense of being in place is bolstered by control of one's life and livelihood. Owning property actually provides a physical location for a person, and this contributes to his sense of being in the right place. Place also has the connotation of position, as within a family, a community, an industry, or some organization. When a person has a sense of being in place, it gives him a sense of order, a sense of security, and a sense of well-being. These, in turn, are essential to creativity and productivity.

The idea that has the world in its grip implicitly aims to destroy this sense of place. This is done by removing the cultural features that the individual relies upon to maintain his sense of well-being. He is forced from his place into some new configuration. The impact of this is to displace people. The degree of the displacement is proportional to the force exerted, but in its subtler dimensions can only occur to people who do not recognize or who fail to resist what is happening to them.

People resist displacement in a variety of ways, but it is no easy matter to resist it. Resistance requires a place to stand and defend.

Greater degrees of displacement make outright resistance difficult, and it becomes precarious or dangerous to resist by confrontation. As displacement becomes more pronounced, people tend to conform outwardly but to resist by evasion and by subtle attempts to manipulate whatever power they may have to their own advantage.

Literal displacement is easy enough to recognize. Figurative displacement, however, is not so readily discerned. After all, if people remain more or less where they have been, how can we tell that they have been displaced? The answer is this: we know it mainly by the way they behave toward the power over them. *People that are being displaced, even when they seem to be at home, attempt to thwart the displacing power by evasion and manipulation.*

As an example, nearly forty years ago Hedrick Smith commented on how Russians living in the former Soviet Union made life tolerable. They evaded, manipulated, and eschewed the political powers in a wide variety of ways. Smith described it this way:

> It fascinated me that there were such cunning devices for foiling the authorities and that Russians, of all people, supposedly being a nation of sheep, would resort to such expedients. For the notion of the totalitarian state, perhaps useful for political scientists as a bird's eye view of Soviet society, misses the human quotient. It conjures up the picture of robots living a regimented existence. Most of the time, it is true, the vast majority of Russians go through the motions of publicly observing the rules. But privately, they are often exerting enormous efforts and practicing uncommon ingenuity to bend or slip through these rules for their own personal ends. 'Slipping through is our national pastime,' a woman lawyer smilingly commented to me.[1]

The same thing is happening now in the United States. The enormous and expanding thrust of the government is something alien to the American people, yet apparently beyond their power to alter. Despite the widespread growth of government and its meddling in ever more details of life, Americans strive mightily to evade the impact of the government's thrust. Indeed, they increasingly attempt to use whatever power and influence they have to manipulate it to their advantage.

While crying out for the need for increased taxes to fund social spending programs to supposedly contribute to the common good, many exert extensive efforts to keep as much of their own income as possible. They pay lawyers, hire tax consultants, tailor their activities, and arrange their accounts and investments so as to pay as little by way of taxes as possible. They seek out investments that will enable them to delay for the longest time the payment of taxes on whatever they have. They use whatever influence they can muster to get as large a tax write-off as possible in their particular undertakings. They work mightily to ensure that their trips have a "business" component, and are thereby tax deductible.

Of course, businesses also go through extensive machinations to reduce their taxes even while spending funds to secure political privileges by lobbying legislators to pass some new law that would provide them some largess. "Tax inversions" are now commonplace, where corporations move official domiciles overseas so as to avoid paying the unusually high U.S. corporate tax rate.

All this wrangling is evidence that people believe that reducing the size of government or even slowing its rate of growth appears futile. The complexity of governmental rules and red tape seems to be an avalanche that cannot be stopped. In fact, many businesspeople have given up efforts to prevent government regulation of their activities. Instead, they exert massive efforts to make these regulations work to their advantage. They collect reams of data and hire lobbyists to influence government policy on their behalf.

In the face of an ever-growing mountain of red tape, citizens ignore or violate the rules and regulations they are supposed to observe. They speed on highways if they believe there are no radar traps, and they quickly fasten seat belts when they spot a police vehicle. They avoid purchasing health insurance if they determine that the penalty for being uninsured is less costly than buying the mandated policy. When a college campus prohibits smoking, the students and faculty light up anyway. They do so secretly and in locations where they are unlikely to be spotted and chastised by "lifestyle police."

There is ample evidence that the practice of evading regulations occurs within the government as well. In the past several years congressional leaders have been charged with drug possession, driving while under the influence, disorderly conduct, and so forth. IRS and Veterans Affairs officials have been investigated for failure to follow their own rules. Moreover, there is plenty of evidence that they routinely abuse the power of their offices. The list of violations is a long one and there is no need for a full recitation here. The point is that legislators and government employees seem no better at following all the rules and regulations than anyone else.

There is an explanation for these developments, for the alienation from government, for the ongoing evasion and manipulation of the law, for the efforts to displace that prompts it all. The explanation can be found in an idea that has become generally accepted. In truth, extraordinary effort is being expended in our age to apply this idea to the whole world. The elective branches of government in the United States have been displaced to a considerable degree by the bureaucracy and the judiciary because of this idea. As the power and sway of government has grown, decision-making has more and more shifted to the more permanent members and branches of government. As the grip of the idea increases, the displacement of all except those who wield power in the name of the idea becomes more pronounced.

What is the idea? Can it be named? That is not so easy to answer. There are names aplenty for the movements spawned by the idea. The most commonly used generic name for the movement in the United States is liberalism, or progressivism. It is also called socialism, or some have called it by the even more inclusive name of collectivism or communitarianism. The more virulent wing of the movement is known as Marxism or communism. Some in the media suggest that we should "lean forward" in pursuit of the idea.

Those writing about the idea may use one or more of the above terms, and may avoid others, but these terms do not name the idea. They actually name methods and emphases, but not the idea that animates them. Even communists refer to socialism as the end and think of it as the idea, but it is not. It is a means, if it is anything. Nothing is more likely than that individuals would confuse these means with the end and the idea. But these things named are the offshoots of the idea and not the idea itself. The idea itself goes unnamed.

The animating idea has no name because there is no name that its adherents accept. The idea is *utopianism*, but there is hardly a person to be found who will acknowledge utopianism as his belief. In common usage, a utopian is one who is impractical and unrealistic. For the proponents of the idea to name it utopianism is to risk trivializing it. If the idea were named utopianism it would become an idea among other ideas. It would become an idea to be examined, to be debated, to be scrutinized, and quite possibly to be refuted.

Such treatment, the proponents of the idea apparently resist. They resist it by focusing upon the method for realizing it rather than the actual animating idea. The idea itself must be an unchallenged good. The animating idea is the root of a secular religion, the leading secular religion of our time. It catches up myriad vague longings set loose by the decline of religion. Or more precisely it provides hope and a faith with credible promises for those who no longer believe the promises of their traditional religions.

The crux of the idea is this: *To achieve maximum human happiness on earth by coordinating the efforts of all people toward that end.* That is, on its face, a most attractive idea. A host of other ideas are clustered around it too, adding to its glow, including such ideas as: harmony, brotherhood, progress, peace, prosperity, comradeship, cooperation, equality, common good, humanitarianism, solidarity, an end to the exploitation of man by man, fulfillment through sharing in a common effort, and so on. Who would deny that it would be good if we would all work together to achieve the maximum happiness of all?

There is, however, a rather large fly in this ointment. In fact, there are several, but let us focus on one. There is bountiful evidence that we are not in agreement as to what would constitute our greatest happiness. One man's delight is often another's torment. One man's exhilaration entails climbing Mount Everest to stand at its crest amidst frigid howling winds in an atmosphere nearly void of oxygen. Another, possibly most of us, would prefer to be at home watching the ascent on television. One man's pleasure is a full stomach after a hearty meal, even if the eventual result is obesity. Another will deny himself perpetually in order to remain slim.

It is not that some of us do not share some of the same or similar preferences. It is rather that if we could be observed in the whole of our being and activity we would be seen to each have an individual pattern whose direction would be to maintain or achieve a sense of our own well-being. These patterns, in turn, give rise both to our achievements and to the conflicts and contests among us. Each of us appears to be determined to pursue his own well-being in his own way. Indeed, the fact that we are self-aware and that we have the power to make choices necessarily results in this pursuit of our individual well-being.

This individuality wreaks havoc on any coordinated effort to achieve collective happiness. Utopians, or whatever they should be called, know this, of course, but they do not accept it as a permanent condition. If they did, they would have to give up their cause as hopeless at the outset. They do not conceive of individuality, this determination to pursue one's own interest in one's own way, as being rooted in human nature and a basic condition of life on this planet. Indeed, except as a figure of speech, they are not inclined to recognize that there is any such thing as human nature. It is just selfishness, they think, a selfishness that is culturally induced.

There are three prongs to the idea that has the world in its grip. The first has already been told: *To achieve maximum human happiness on earth by coordinating the efforts of all people toward that end.* The second is now before us, and can be stated in this way: *We must root out, discredit, and discard all aspects of culture that play any role in inducing or supporting the individual's pursuit of his own self-interest.* The corollary of this is that *an ethos that focuses attention on what is supposed to be the common good of humanity must be developed.*

It is easy for people to be unaware of how radical this idea really is. For one thing, we have become acclimated to many ideas associated with it. For example, socialism is the main political tool for accomplishing the imagined end and it has become increasingly accepted by people around the world. In lands where the march to socialism is gradual, such as the United States, it is often not admittedly linked to any ideology. If it were called socialism, there are many who would reject it outright. The whole pattern of activity associated with socialism is not perceived as stemming from the idea, because the idea itself remains unnamed. Yet, if it were recognized for what it is, it would probably not be possible to conceive a more radical idea than that of rooting out or altering everything in the culture that is individualistic.

Socialism is sometimes defined as the public ownership of the means of the production and distribution of goods and services. But the idea that has the world in its grip, an idea that for practical purposes may be called socialism, does not simply entail the alteration of ownership; it entails the alteration of the whole cultural environment.

The reason for this is because many people do not readily submit themselves and their aims in life to the ideal of the idea. For the idea to succeed, everyone must work together toward its end. As such, anyone who is not committed to the idea must be transformed so that they accept it willingly. There is an old formulation that people live in a world where there is both nature and nurture. According to the proponents of the idea, human nature does not really exist. There remains only nurture. The person is defined completely by the culture that nurtures him. And it is this culture that champions individuality that must be destroyed and replaced with a culture that nurtures individuals to see the need for the coordination of all human effort as the ultimate truth. As we will see, this is happening all around us.

This brings us to the third prong of the idea. It is this: *Government is the primary instrument to be used to accomplish the necessary destruction or alteration of culture, because government allows us to introduce force.* Some explanation is warranted here. The very attractiveness of the idea is that men must long to coordinate their efforts to achieve joy and happiness. Why then should force be introduced into the equation? The answer is that it is introduced out of necessity. The bent of all people is to pursue their own self-interest. It is such an integral part of the human condition that proponents of the idea assert that only government can get rid of it. Force must be used to free men from the hold of selfishness.

This, then, is a distillation of all three prongs of the idea that holds the world in its grip: *To use government to coordinate all efforts toward realizing maximum happiness on this earth, and to root out and destroy all that stands in the way.*

There are various particular articulations of the idea, but the important point is that they all arise from a certain root idea. They arise from a vision of the achievement of joy and happiness through a coordinated effort by everyone to achieve it. Success hinges upon destroying or altering any culture of traditional values and norms, especially when these values champion individualism in any form.

Evidence for these assertions has not yet been provided. That will be the quest for the rest of this book. We aim to provide as much evidence as needed to make the case. Still, the idea must be clear from the beginning. A great deal of energy has gone into confusing and obscuring the nature of socialism. In some countries, socialism's advocates never link measures and activities to their ultimate ideology. Thus, if connections are to be shown, it must be understood from the beginning what is to be connected. The connection is between the root idea and the great variety of socialist efforts going on in the world.

The idea that has the world in its grip is a totalitarian idea. It does not appear that way in a good many nations as of yet. It may never proceed to that point in some places, but that does not keep it from being a totalitarian idea. Totalitarianism is implicit in the idea. An absolute, dictatorial government is necessary if the individual is to be fitted into the imagined utopia. If all constructive activity could be coordinated to the end of achieving happiness, everyone would be under the sway of the coordinating force. Whether it would achieve happiness or not would be a moot question, for there would be no independent judgment to determine whether it was happiness or universal torment. According to the idea the very condition of independence must be discarded so that complete coordination of the social good can be realized. The advancement of the idea, then, is the advancement toward totalitarianism.

Even so, this fact is not the connection or the impact that will occupy most of our attention. Nowhere has there been sufficient success in applying the idea such that the efforts of all people could be said to have been coordinated. What has happened, and is happening, is a struggle throughout the nations of the world where efforts have been made to apply the idea. It is a struggle between men bent on pursuing their own self-interest and the governments who are attempting to make them serve some other interest. It is the great undeclared war. It is a war in which many of those most tenaciously defending themselves in private openly profess the social emphasis of the government in their public pronouncements. It is, in its deeper dimensions, the struggle of those being displaced against their displacers.

The impact that shall most occupy our attention is displacement. The attempt to remove the basis of individuality is displayed for us as an assault upon the inherited culture. Indeed, all that has been inherited from the past becomes suspect to those under the sway of the idea. The received social arrangements, the place of men in society, the place of women in society, the religious tradition, the definition of marriage, customs, habits, and ways of acting, everything that could conceivably give support to individuality must be attacked. The result is displacement. Many Americans have sensed this displacement for a long time. They have probably not understood that it is a necessary tactic to lay the groundwork for more widespread acceptance of the idea in America.

Any man's sense of place is culturally (as socialists use the word) derived. It relies upon continuity with the past. Family ties, duties, obligations, and achievements buttress it. His property, his savings, that which is owed to him and that which he owes, all give him his place. The teachings of his childhood have helped to form him. His religion may well provide him with transcendental support for his beliefs. A part of a person's definition as a being is that of being either male or female, and the role this infers upon us. All the familiar adjuncts of his being—music, paintings, books, working instruments, language, furniture, and what not—are cultural artifacts that confirm and bolster his place.

The thrust of revolution in our time (and gradualism is piecemeal revolution) is not simply to divest us of ownership or of control of our property. It is that, of course, but it is so much more. It is to divest us of our received culture. It is to break the ties that bind the members of family to one another. It is to sever religion from education. It is to interpenetrate every relationship with the power of the state, not in support of the individual but to have the relation determined by social imperatives. It is to so alter the familiar adjuncts to our being that they are no longer ours but belong to something beyond us. It is to blur the distinctions between male and female, to cut away the authority of culture, and to leave us naked.

The near perfect symbol of what is aimed at is public nudity. Clothes do serve some useful purposes: to keep us warm in colder climates, to shield us from the burning rays of the sun in others, and to provide us with pockets that are convenient places to store odds and ends. Aside from that, though, clothes are emblems of all the received culture by which we maintain our privacy, define our status, and establish our independent realm. To be naked in public means to be exposed and helpless. Our last defenses are gone; we are at the mercy of all who behold us. Similarly, the removal of cultural protection is the prelude to tyranny.

The idea that has the world in its grip tends to make all of us displaced persons. It does so because it fuels the assault on culture, upon religion and morality, and upon civilization itself. As these are taken away, or lose their vitality, men even lose the means by which they can defend themselves. In some places the displacement has been dramatic and drastic. In others the displacement is more gradual and has not yet assumed the outward appearance of direct brutality. The more thoroughly the idea is applied, however, the more the grip will tighten.

The world is not, however, simply in the grip of a general idea. It is in the grip of variations in the application of the idea from country to country, as these have been shaped by a variety of leaders from different backgrounds. We must turn now to an unpacking of the idea to expose it more thoroughly and to particular developments and applications of it.

Two

Revolutionary vs. Evolutionary Socialism

> Both for the production on a mass scale of this communist consciousness, and for the success of the cause itself, the alteration of men on a mass scale is necessary, an alteration which can only take place in a practical movement, a *revolution*; this revolution is necessary, therefore, not only because the *ruling* class cannot be overthrown in any other way, but also because the class *overthrowing* it can only in a revolution succeed in ridding itself of all the muck of ages and become fitted to found society anew.
> — Karl Marx, *The German Ideology*[2]

The idea that has the world in its grip has one essential political tool that has two poles. One pole is the revolutionary road to socialism; the other is the evolutionary road to socialism. Despite the horrendous failure of the implementation of socialism under either pole, proponents of the idea continue to cling to their use. Indeed, they have no choice since socialism, broadly defined, is their only political tool.

The idea—to achieve maximum happiness on this earth by coordinating all human efforts toward its realization—is the same motivating factor for both poles. Both operate to root out and destroy the received culture and use government as the instrument that is supposed to help achieve the realization of the goal. The basic difference is one of tactics. And tactics are no small matter when the question is whether "persuasion" is best accomplished by a shot in the back of the head or through some other mechanism.

Revolutionary Socialism

It is best to begin the examination of particular approaches to socialism with Marxism. While few countries now claim to be "communist," all modern socialism comes into focus most clearly when seen from the angle of Marxism. It has been said that all of Western philosophy is a series of footnotes to Plato. It can be said with equal validity that all of modern socialism is a series of footnotes to Karl Marx.

Why this should be so is a baffling question. Marx was certainly not a leader of men. Most people disliked him, even if he did not reciprocate in kind. He championed the cause of the laborer (or industrial proletariat, as he chose to call him), yet he was himself an intellectual. He proclaimed the importance of action, yet he spent much of his life in libraries amidst the musty smell of books. His ghost hovers over the thrust toward planned economies for nations and empires, yet he was throughout his life incompetent to manage his own financial affairs. Even his literary output fell short of his aims and the expectations of those who provided financial aid. He is best known for *The Communist Manifesto*, a rather short pamphlet that was the joint effort with Friedrich Engels, with whom he also produced one volume of *Das Kapital*. Most of his other writing was done in spurts, and consisted mainly of critiques of other contemporary papers, articles, and books. There was much more of what was wrong with the thinking of others than there was of straightforward development of his ideas.

The details of his life go further toward explaining why he may have held certain beliefs than toward accounting for why others were attracted by the Marxian formulations. Marx was, for most of his adult life, a man without a country, if country be taken to mean not only a nation but also religion, culture, and a sense of being a part of a received heritage. Marx's father and mother had been Jewish. However, his father, it was said, converted to Christianity to keep his government job. Karl Marx was baptized a Lutheran but in early manhood became a militant atheist.

He attended universities at Bonn and Berlin, but presented his doctoral thesis for his degree to the University of Jena, which he had never attended. He never had what could be called a regular job but earned such income as he did from writing and editorial work. Though he married and fathered several children, the family moved from place to place as Marx sought refuge first here, then there. He was frequently in trouble with the political authorities for his revolutionary activity, seeking refuge in Paris, in Brussels, and finally in London. Such friends as he had were fellow revolutionaries, and, among them, he got along only with those who agreed with his version of things. His country, if he had one, was in his mind, and that does help to explain his doctrines.

What is Marxism? One way to answer the question is to say that it is that body of doctrines that was formulated by Karl Marx in collaboration with Friedrich Engels in the course of both of their lives. (Engels outlived Marx by several years and continued to expand upon the work that Marx had done.) Or, it can be approached from the angle of its antecedents in German romanticism, Hegelianism, the materialism of Feuerbach, the socialism of Proudhon, the anarchism of Bakunin, and the whole complex of mid-nineteenth century radicalism that was nipping and yapping at European society. Or, it can be traced forward in time into Leninism, Stalinism, Maoism, and all the variants of it that have been shaped by men attempting to apply it or apply some variety of it.

But any or all of these approaches would take us away from, rather than toward, the core of Marxism. It is misleading, too, to treat Marxism as a system of thought. It is certainly not a system of thought by reason of fitting into the established categories for utilizing reason and experience. Marx did not proceed deductively from self-evident axioms. Nor did he proceed inductively to arrive at conclusions from the assembled evidence.

If it were a system of thought, it could be tested and found to be true or false. It could be held up against actuality and be refuted. Bertram D. Wolfe noted that Marxism "cannot be shaken by mere rational or factual refutation of any number of its concrete propositions, even those that are central to its logical structure."[3] There may be several reasons for this, but a crucial one has not been much emphasized. Marx is not talking about actuality, or what we ordinarily call reality, in his basic propositions. It is difficult to appeal to reality in an effort to refute that which bears no demonstrable relation to it.

Marx's mode of arriving at conclusions needs to be illustrated by example to show that he was not operating in contact with reality. This may be done best by his labor theory of value, which is the lynchpin of Marxism. Marx tells us, first, that the value of commodities is determined by the amount of labor used in making them. He put it this way: "The relative values of commodities are, therefore, determined by the respective quantities or amounts of labour, worked up, realized, fixed in them."[4] But it is not as simple as that might sound. Marx hastens to assure us that "there exists no such thing as the Value of Labour in the common acceptance of the word."[5] And, what the working man sells, he says, is not labor but "Labouring Power." And there is another difficulty to be got out of the way, too. It might be supposed from Marx's initial formulation that the more work that went into a commodity the more it would be worth. Not at all, says Marx. It is not labor per se that determines value, but the amount of "social labour" that goes into making a product.

We could try to follow Marx's analysis further, but it is not necessary. Marx claims to be talking about the real world. He is not. Every key word and phrase he uses is loaded with his own special meaning. All his certainty is reserved for those concepts he has given his own special meaning. Value is not something that arises from our desires. Labor is not labor, it is "labouring power." The amount of labor that matters is not just labor, it is "social labour," whatever that is.

How do we know that the value of a commodity is determined by the amount of social labor in it? We know it, if we know it at all, only because Marx has told us. There are no calculations that can be performed to prove it. After all, labor that can be quantified by adding up hours and minutes is not what matters; it is social labor that, according to Marx, determines value.

Marxism is an anti-religious religion. To see it in any other light is to miss its character and appeal. A lifelong student of Marxism describes it this way:

> In an age prepared for by nearly two thousand years of Christianity with its millennial expectations, when the faith of millions has grown dim, and the altar seems vacant of its image, Marxism has arisen to offer a fresh, antireligious religion, a

new faith, passionate and demanding, a new vision of the Last Things, a new Apocalypse, and a new Paradise.⁶

Karl Marx was a poet and a prophet—a poor poet and false prophet, no doubt, but poet and prophet nonetheless. Not nearly enough has been made of the poetic flavor of Marx's writing. This is not surprising, for few undertakings are as removed from poetry as economics, particularly the ponderous variety of economics constructed by Marx. Yet many of the Marxian formulations are best grasped as the work of a poet. Take the following, for example:

> The task of history, once the world beyond truth has disappeared, is to establish the truth of this world. The immediate task of philosophy that is at the service of history, once the saintly form of human self-alienation has been unmasked, is to unmask self-alienation in its unholy forms. Thus the criticism of heaven turns into the criticism of the earth, the criticism of religion into the criticism of right, and the criticism of theology into the criticism of politics.⁷

Whether any sense can be made of this passage is a question that can be left to the side. If anything can be made of it, it is in the manner of an obscure poem. What is "the world beyond truth," or "the truth of this world," or "the saintly form of self-alienation," or "the criticism of heaven"? One could be forgiven for concluding that the whole passage is nonsense.

Marx was a prophet too. Not a prophet of God, of course, but a prophet of History. He was the John the Baptist of communism, traveling hither and yon to proclaim the imminent coming of the Revolution. Everywhere Marx looked he saw paradox, contradiction, struggle, and eventual destruction. Disharmony prevailed everywhere, a disharmony that was fated to continue and worsen until an ultimate event would occur that would bring an end to it and produce harmony and unity. The key concepts of the Marxian ideology are these: *alienation, class struggle, industrial proletariat, bourgeoisie, labor theory of value, capitalism, social revolution, socialism,* and *communism.*

Marx was an intellectual scavenger, taking in vast quantities of literature by his voluminous reading, opposing the particulars of almost every formulation he encountered, then subjecting all to his own particular turn of mind before he appeared in print with the result. He defined his position in opposition to what he read, but he also incorporated much of what he read into his position.

Crucial to Marxian ideology is Marx's theory of alienation. The theory of alienation was most fully developed in his earlier writings, and there is some tendency to discount it because some of these early writings were not published until long after his death. The theory goes like this: Man as we know him is not real, essential man. His reason is flawed. What he experiences is distorted by ideology. He is not free but is rather imprisoned by circumstances and conditions over which he has no control.

He is alienated from himself, first of all, by religion. Religion subjects him to the mediating powers of others. He is alienated from himself by private property. Property sets him at odds with others and alienates him from his social nature. He is alienated from himself by the state. The state is an artificial creature that arises from division into classes in society. It is an instrument of class rule. He is alienated from the product of his labor by its appropriation by the capitalist. This alienation is apparently exacerbated by the division of labor.

The last proposition is most familiar in the form of the alienation of the wage earner from the product his labor. Marx and Engels placed the greatest emphasis upon it. Here is a fairly typical expression of the alienation of the worker theory (again, with a characteristic poetic flair):

> The alienation of the worker in his object is expressed as follows in the laws of political economy: the more the worker produces the less he has to consume; the more value he creates the more worthless he becomes; the more refined his product the more crude and misshapen the worker; the more civilized the product the more barbarous the worker.[8]

It was his version of "alienation" that made revolution necessary for Marx. Marx was certainly aware that during his lifetime governments were taking various measures intended to improve the lot of the worker. Why might socialism not be achieved by gradual degrees in an evolutionary fashion? Marx sometimes wavered on the matter, but he returned again and again to the position that revolution will be necessary. It will be necessary because alienation is too broadly and deeply established.

What Marx meant by revolution, as is often the case in his special language, is given a special meaning. One thing he meant was a conflict in which the industrial proletariat should triumph over the bourgeoisie. Marx and Engels put it this way:

> The immediate aim of the Communists is the same as that of all the other proletarian parties: formation of the proletariat into a class, overthrow of the bourgeois supremacy, conquest of the political power by the proletariat.[9]

As a result of the revolution everything, *everything*, is to be altered and changed: "The Communists disdain to conceal their views and aims. They openly declare that their ends can be attained only by the forcible overthrow of all existing social conditions."[10] Everything is to be transformed:

> Communism is the positive abolition of private property and thus of human self-alienation and therefore the real appropriation of the human essence by and for the man. This is communism as the complete and conscious return of man.... It is the genuine resolution of the antagonism between man and nature and between man and man. It is the true resolution of the struggle between existence and essence, between objectification and self-affirmation, between freedom and necessity, between individual and species.[11]

According to Marx all existing relations must be abolished—destroyed so that social man may emerge:

> Religion, family, state, law, morality, science and art are only particular forms of production and fall under its general law. The positive abolition of private property and the appropriation of human life is therefore the positive abolition of all alienation, thus the return of man out of religion, family, state, etc., into his human, i.e. social, being.[12]

Marx apparently realized that such a revolution would not be completed swiftly. He said that the working class 'will have to pass through long struggles, through a series of historic processes, transforming circumstances and men.'[13]

The remainder of the Marxian formulations are mainly an attempt to establish the "scientific" necessity of the revolution. The labor theory of value was the lynchpin of this demonstration. If Marx was right in this theory, the laboring man was being robbed of the fruits of his labor. Moreover, he claimed that the more capital that was accumulated, invested, and concentrated, the more deplorable would be the plight of the industrial worker. More and more people would fall into this class; in numbers it would constitute the majority of people in a country. When the situation of the working class became sufficiently desperate, its numbers so overwhelming, it would revolt and overthrow the ruling class. All of history had been a series of class struggles. Marx proclaimed that the stage was being set for the final class struggle, the class struggle to end all class struggles; the class struggle between the proletariat and the bourgeoisie.

It is often alleged that the tyranny of communism in practice is the result of some sort of aberration from Marxism. On the contrary, the tyranny is implicit in the ideology. A review of the essentials of Marxism should demonstrate why this is so.

The engine of Marxism is hatred—hatred for everything as it is, hatred of religion, hatred of the division of labor, hatred of the state, hatred of capitalists, and hatred of private property. Above all, Marxism is a hatred of the past, everything shaped out of it, everything drawn from it, which is to say, just about everything. In short, Marxism hates man as he is and has been.

The *modus operandi* of Marxism is destruction. That is the true meaning of Marxian revolution. It is no simple seizure of political power. It might better be conceived of as a cataclysmic earthquake, followed by devastating tremor after devastating tremor until every relationship is broken. All that has been accumulated through the ages must be destroyed—property relationships, religious belief, family ties, legal forms, the intellectual heritage, culture and civilization itself. How else, but by tyranny, can such a destruction be wrought?

Tyranny is embedded in the very framework of Marxism. According to him the course of history is determined. It has a direction that is beyond our control. Such history is not a guide, but a dictator, so to speak. More, "History is the judge—its executioner, the proletarian."[14]

The executioner and tyrant is not the whole body of the proletariat; it is to be carried out by the class-conscious wing. No clearer prescription for tyranny has been contrived.

On the other side of the divide, Marx tells us that all this will end. The class struggle will end with the victory of the proletariat. The state will be no more; it will wither away. The dictatorship of the proletariat will have ended because its work will be done. Man will no longer be separated from man; he will have become completely social. He will have become pure man, so to speak, with all his energies released and himself integrated. Even the rift between man and nature will be healed.

The appeal of Marxism lies in the fact that it justifies and sanctifies the release of demonic urges in each of us. It justifies and sanctifies hate, envy, the love of power, the bent to destruction, the desire to set everything right (particularly others), and all the vague and unfulfilled longings of man. It offers to the believer the assurance of final victory. It offers an end to the struggle that has been man's lot throughout history. Its deepest appeal has always been to intellectuals, to those men who sit on the fringes of society with their ideas. It holds out to them the hope and expectation that their ideas can at last become actuality.

Evolutionary Socialism

Karl Marx and Friedrich Engels staked out the revolutionary road to socialism; but there is another road to socialism, one that is much more prevalent than the revolutionary path. The evolutionary road draws sustenance from Marxism. But evolutionary socialism has its own ideology, and it needs to be examined on its own grounds.

The appeal of Marxism to intellectuals has been noted often. A part of the reason for this is no particular mystery. Marxism holds out to the intellectual the hope of escape from one of his most persistent frustrations. An intellectual is, by definition, one who is devoted to ideas, their formulation and exposition. But ideas are only completed or fulfilled when they are put into practice. At least this is so for some ideas, particularly those having to do with social change. Therein, however, lies the source of frustration for modern intellectuals: their ideas are often denied any impact on society. They fill the pages of books but do not go into practice.

Karl Marx projected a vision of a dramatic ending of this state of affairs. Come the revolution, he claimed, the ideas would become actuality. The frustration of the intellectual would presumably end; for he would no longer have a conception of a world different from the world he would be experiencing.

There is a deeper reason for the appeal of Marxism to intellectuals or else it would never have gained the hold that it has had. It is that man needs an explanation of the world in which he lives. He wants to know where it came from and where it is going. Above all, he needs a purpose in life, a purpose that goes beyond him but with which he can identify and find meaning. He needs, in a word, religion. But many intellectuals cut themselves loose from the traditional religions. They ignore religion or become agnostics or atheists, quite often of the most militant variety. Marxism supplies for them the place that religion has usually held for most men.

Of course, Marxism is not scientific. Neither the economic analysis nor the historical prediction can pass muster as science. They are a compound of special pleading and wishful thinking. The very appeal of Marxism lies in the fact that to believe it requires an act of faith, as does any religion. The intellectual of the appropriate temperament finds in the Marxist religion hope for the hopeless, meaning in history, the promised resolution of all conflict, and the expectation of union, even communion with all men.

Marxism is the religion of socialism. Many intellectuals are attracted to this anti-religious religion. Many of those attracted to it are not communists, but rather have turned to one of the other varieties of socialism.

It is tempting to deal with socialism as being watered-down Marxism. There is some substance to this view. As stated earlier, Marxism is the most virulent branch of socialism. When any other approach to socialism is compared with the revolutionary approach it pales beside it. More, the man who gave currency to the phrase, "evolutionary socialism," Eduard Bernstein, is usually classified as a revisionist Marxist.

It may be most helpful to think of revolutionary and evolutionary socialism as belonging to the same family but being different species. Undoubtedly, they share common traits, as do members of a biological family. But they are sufficiently different from one another to be thought of as different species. The basic idea from which they spring is the same, but the articulation of it is distinctly different. An evolutionary socialist may approve a revolution somewhere or other, but he does not become himself a revolutionist. In like manner a revolutionary socialist may approve, even work to bring about, some government intervention, but remain, all the while, a convinced revolutionist.

There are three main components in evolutionary socialist tactics. All three distinguish them from Marxism in theory, and at least two of them are real differences. They are *gradualism*, *democracy*, and *statism*.

In contrast to the revolution of communism, gradualism is a process whereby socialism occurs slowly over time, step by step. Gradualism links the movement toward socialism and the idea of evolutionary progress. Thus, gradualism is related to theories of biological evolution. Following this junction, socialism is the goal, gradualism the way, and evolutionary progress the engine to get there.

Gradualists propose that movement toward socialism is progress, not as a proposition in need of proof, but rather as a definitive statement of fact. And the notion that movement toward socialism is progress has served them well. It enables them to claim that all acts moving in their direction are progressive, while any steps in the other direction are degenerating and retrogressive.

Revolutionists and gradualists are likely to disagree as to whether socialists should participate in a bourgeois government. Should socialists participate in the system? By participating in it, are they not giving tacit approval to it? The pure revolutionists tend to answer that they would. The state—and most emphatically, the bourgeois state—is the enemy. Democratic socialists take the other side, and are willing to participate in the government.

Evolutionary socialists might be referred to as being "pragmatic." They are not wedded to any particular means in the achievement of power and the enactment of their policies. Hence, democracy may mean for them majority rule when they have a majority. On the other hand, it may mean equality when they are pressing for something other than a parliamentary device for the achievement of their ends. Methods do not matter so long as they are collectivist in principle. Collectivism is the principle, and democracy the means.

Finally, evolutionary socialism is statist. It determinedly uses the power of government for its purposes. This provides another distinction between evolutionary and revolutionary socialism. The difference is part theoretical and part the role that government is supposed to play and how it is to be done. In theory, Marxists are not statists. The State, according to Marx, was supposed to wither away under communism. By way of contrast, evolutionists use the existing state and work within it to achieve their collectivist vision.

The tactics of socialists differ much from country to country. In those nations where socialism is avowed as a desirable goal, it is sometimes sufficient that some policies be adopted because they are required by socialism. In countries, such as the United States, where a relatively few of the advocates avow their socialism, policies are promoted on other grounds. In the United States those who are at the forefront in pushing the gradualist type of reforms are most often referred to as "liberals" or as "progressives." They will typically present themselves as either one depending on which term is most acceptable at the time they use it.

The amazing thing is the continuing impetus toward socialism and the remarkable consistency in what is sought from land to land. Despite even the most obvious failures, despite political setbacks from time to time, despite cultural differences from one nation to another, the impetus rises again and again and the same sorts of measures continue to be enacted.

The question must arise as to where and what is the source of this impetus and consistency. With evolutionary socialism there is no institution with either the power or authority to promulgate a party line across the boundaries of nations. Even within countries, there is usually no authoritative group to enforce some party line. The notion that it is done by some international cabal is appealing, but such organizations as exist lack the power and authority to promote socialism that thoroughly.

The answer, as we have explored it thus far, is this: The world is in the grip of an idea. The idea is: *To use government to coordinate all efforts toward realizing maximum happiness on this earth, and to root out and destroy all that stands in the way.* Believers in the idea put their faith in progress, in collectivist democracy, and in the possibility of changing human nature so as to eventually coordinate all efforts behind the movement.

To the have-nots, to the down-and-outs, to any who conceive that they have not received a fair share (and the number of these is enormous) socialism promises that all this will be changed. Socialists hold up a vision of perfection beside the realities of an imperfect world and proclaim that they know how to attain the perfection.

The discussion of revolutionary and evolutionary socialism has one main purpose here. It is to show the connection between the ideas and the practices. Socialists of whatever persuasion focus attention upon and talk most about economic matters. They proclaim that the ills that beset us are economic in origin. But the task that they propose to undertake does not simply involve rearranging economies. An economy does not exist in lofty isolation from man, society, morality, religion, culture, habits, customs, and traditions.

Indeed, economy is what it is because man is what he is. This being so, anyone attempting to institute new and different economic arrangements must also devise a new man, new society, new morality, and so on. It may be less painful to go about it gradually rather than in one fell swoop, but it finally must be done whichever way is taken. The damage must be done because the old man, the old society, the old morality, and so on, must be rooted out, altered, or destroyed. The evolutionary approach is subtle because much of the process is hidden beneath diversionary arguments and gradual methods. It is there, nonetheless.

The impact of the thrust toward socialism is to destroy the independence of the individual and leave him exposed to the power of government and the influence of whoever has it or will wield it. This is so because the thrust of socialism is to remove all the supports by which he may stand as an individual: the supports of a free society, of morality, of religion, of custom and of tradition. The logic of this development is inherent within the socialist idea.

Three

The Need to Deceive

This story is said to have been told by a man who served many years ago as a tour guide in and around Detroit, Michigan. It was the height of American auto manufacturing in that city. One day the tour guide was assigned to show Ford's River Rouge plant to a group of visiting Russian engineers. The guide noted that they were soon in a jovial mood, laughing, talking, and generally in a festive spirit. Just as they passed a huge parking lot filled with cars, they became even more animated. The one who spoke the best English asked the guide this question:

'Do they prepare themselves like this to impress all their visitors? Or is it just for us?'
'What do you mean?' the guide asked.
'The impressive number of cars. It's a flattering illustration of Ford's capacity for production.'
The guide pointed out that Ford would hardly have arranged such a display since it was the employee's parking lot and the cars in question were used by and belonged to them. Furthermore, he pointed out that they must have noticed the abundance of automobiles on the streets and highways of the city and that the automobile was the individual's chief means of transportation. But this answer did not satisfy the Russian's inquiry.
'You're kidding,' he said, 'so many cars?'

Nevertheless, the guide continued to point to the fact that these were the employees' cars and that all they needed to do to prove it was to ask the employees. The Russian declared that such a notion was typical propaganda and that asking the employees would prove nothing.

'We know that old trick. The plant is well prepared for our visit. Every worker has learned by heart how to answer our questions. Unless he wants to be fired or arrested he'll give the proper answer.'

Frustrated at his inability to convince the Russian of the true nature of the situation the guide resorted to a last effort. Why don't we just wait here until the shift change and you can see for yourselves who owns the cars? But the Russian was only amused.

'What do you take me for,' he asked, 'an idiot? It's simple to stage such a show. I don't hold Americans for bunglers. If you do something, you do it well. You are a big nation, and you know how to deal with other nations.'[15]

Nothing could convince the Russian that it was not a show staged for their benefit.

Variations of this story have been told many times. Such stories were sometimes told to illustrate the disparity between the material condition of former Soviet workers and those in the United States. That was undoubtedly an important point, but that is not the point we want to emphasize here. The story was also told to point out the lengths that Soviet communists went to in arranging the itineraries of visitors to their country so as to give them the impression that things were going very well there. This is nearer to the point we wish to make here, but that too does not capture all that is involved.

What is most important is the impact of the idea, which held the Russian Empire in its grip for over seventy years. Communism deliberately hid behind a façade. Likewise, by its very nature, all forms of socialism must hide the reality of what it actually does behind a variety of façades. The Russian form of socialism provided the most extensive façade that any nation had ever erected. Every effort was made to put the best face on the practice of communism even though the truth was far afield. The extensive nature of the façade is the reason why our introductory story was so often repeated. The Russian people were so familiar with the extent of the Soviet government's effort to deceive people that they readily believed that Ford Motor Company too would participate in creating its own façade to deceive a few visiting engineers.

There are two common ways of misinterpreting communist deceptions. One is mistaking the façade for the reality of communism. The literature produced during the Soviet Union's existence provides ample evidence of this error. Numerous people returned from short visits to that land with favorable accounts of what they saw. Of course, the credibility of those accounts depended upon accepting the façade as the whole of the reality of the Soviet situation. The other misinterpretation comes from those who grasped the dimensions of the façade and perceived a gigantic hypocrisy that produced it. Such hypocrisy, they concluded, could only mean that communism was a sham and that its practitioners were hypocritically hiding their lust for power behind an ideological mask. But this conclusion misplaces cause and effect.

Deception *is the effect* of the communist ideology. The same is true for all forms of socialism, which must at points hide behind some kind of deception. The love of power resides in every human breast whether that love is dormant or active. When given the opportunity to gain it and wield it without hindrance, it is always a problem. That problem is compounded by the idea. Socialist ideology is not a mask; it is a cause. It is the cause that has produced the effects of deception. Before explaining why this is the case, it is perhaps worthwhile to consider the dimensions of the façade as it was constructed in the former Soviet Union. This will give us insight into the various deceptions being constructed by socialist governments worldwide. Such deceptions are also increasingly fabricated in the United States.

The Soviet government itself was a façade. It was an elaborate structure that bore no relation whatsoever to the way in which decisions were made or to who exercised power and control. In theory, the power of government was supposed to be vested in the Supreme Soviet that was composed of the Council of the Union and the Council of the Nationalities. The members for these were chosen by popular election. When the Supreme Soviet was not in session, which was most of the time, its functions fell to an executive body called the Presidium. On the surface, this seemed very democratic.

In truth, the Supreme Soviet was only window dressing, so to speak. It merely approved decisions that had already been made. Moreover, those who were actually in charge had already preselected those chosen as candidates for membership in the body and they ran for their offices unopposed. In reality, the people voting had no voice at all in what government did. The actual power was to be held in the Communist Party whose membership numbered in the millions but made up a small fraction of the total population. In addition, the real power rested at the top of this organization in the *Politburo*. It was composed of approximately sixteen people, but was typically directed by the arbitrary dictates of the person at the top, as in the case of Joseph Stalin.

The governmental structure of the Soviet Union was clearly nothing more than a series of façades. Popular elections were of no value at all. The Supreme Soviet, the supposed legislative body, had no real power. The Party, too, was a façade. It presented itself as the seat of power, but that was merely a symbol and not the ultimate source of power. Even the Politburo was a bit of a façade as its members typically had to submit to the will of the single man in charge.

Behind all the façades is the ideology. In practice this ideology can only be driven and personified by the action of the one man in charge. Further, there can be only one man in charge for he must set forth the "correct" interpretation of the ideology. It is expected that the party members must then embrace this vision or be subject to expulsion, or worse. Such party rule is the norm wherever the idea that has the world in its grip has been most fully embraced. It is rule by an idea.

All forms of socialism operate behind a cover of words. For example, the Soviet Union was supposedly founded on a constitution. During its existence there were several such documents written. But they too were but façades. According to any sensible definition constitutions are documents that set forth the power of government. They prescribe both the powers and limitations of government. They set out who is qualified to govern and how they are to be selected. Moreover, they provide procedures by which the government operates. They may affirm certain rights belonging to the people as well as the limitations and restrictions imposed on the government. While the Soviet constitutions appeared to do these things, the truth was quite the opposite. The constitutions written were purely ideological in nature. As such, the documents were merely another façade aimed at masking the true nature of government.

In addition to all of these façades, and despite the fact that they were atheists, the Soviet communists went to great lengths to maintain the Orthodox Christian Church. You would have thought that they would have simply closed down all the churches. Indeed, many church buildings were converted to museums and the church itself was gutted of its Christian message. However, not all the churches were closed and its official presence was never eradicated. Instead, its clergy were often employed to inform on local members. In some cases the churchmen were even members of the secret police.

Beyond its use of the church, the communists also wanted to present the notion that all people were equal. As such, women were often employed in lines of work that were traditionally performed by men and party members were expected to dress so as not to stand out in public. But, once again, this was a façade as Party members had access to special privileges that were unavailable to the average person and women still had to fulfill the traditional roles of housework within the family.

Why all these, and other façades? Why did they erect elaborate governmental structures that did not govern? Why the pretense of democracy? Why have extensive electoral campaigns when the results of the election were a foregone conclusion? Why bother to tally the votes when the electorate had no choice? Why have written constitutions when they neither inhibited those who ruled nor assured benefits to the ruled? Why would an atheist regime attempt to have a church serve as a façade? Why did the regime maintain a façade of equality when everywhere great inequalities prevailed? Why create model kindergartens, collective farms, prisons, and industrial plants? In short, why erect façade after façade at such a tremendous effort and expense? Who were they trying to impress?

It was widely believed that these façades were erected mainly to impress foreigners so as to conceal the reality of the economic ineptness of socialism. Undoubtedly, this was one of the reasons for which such façade building took place. For example the façade that there was freedom of religion was mainly done for foreign consumption. Surely, too, were the façades of foreign diplomacy that the Soviet Union erected to conceal the activities of their secret police in other lands. It was always important to the Soviet leaders to present a favorable impression to foreigners. The apparent success of socialism and communism was essential to the spread of the idea. If the ideology of communism was the wave of the future it needed to look attractive to anyone considering traveling down that path. Especially since the truth would repel any decent person.

But the façades were not just for the benefit of foreigners. They were for the inhabitants of the Soviet Union as well. How, it may be asked, could they have been for the people who were least likely to be fooled for long by them? After all, the people forced to live with the depressing results of actual communism knew better. However, it is still possible to be impressed by façades even if one is not misled by them. People are typically thrilled and horrified by movies depicting catastrophes even though they know that they are not witnessing actual catastrophes. It was an impressive feat that the Soviets could garner a near unanimous vote of the electorate even though the election was rigged. In spite of the fact that the powers that be put up only one candidate, the vast majority of the people still dutifully went to the polls to cast their votes for this candidate. Why bother?

Underlying all the explanations of why the Russians created these façades is something deeper. All forms of socialism are mired in the need to deceive. The idea itself is a deception. Any effort to impose it can only be maintained by erecting façade after façade. Façades are the natural fruit of deception. Socialism in any of its forms cannot produce the freedom that it promises. It cannot produce a democratic society and it cannot transform mankind. It cannot direct all human effort to its goal of creating paradise on earth. Marxian ideology is a kind of poetic vision of man, society, economics, and life, which does not now, never did, and never will exist in the world as it is. There simply is no reason whatsoever to believe that its aims could ever be realized. All the efforts to bring the vision into being have resulted in something very different from what was promised. Therefore, it is only possible to create illusions that it works.

Socialism, broadly defined, is not basically a social system, an economic system, or even a political system. Fundamentally, it is a *conspiracy*. It presents itself to the world as a conspiracy to gain, hold, and wield power to effect a great transformation. But in its inward parts, so to speak, it is a conspiracy to deceive and an agreement to be deceived.

Who does it deceive? The answer is that it aims to deceive everyone who needs to be deceived by it. All who accept it, who work to apply it, who aid it in any way, or on whom it is being imposed, need to be deceived. Even those most deeply involved in creating the deception need to be deceived. Indeed, they have the greatest need to be deceived, because they have the greatest need to believe in it.

In the former Soviet Union those in the Politburo had the greatest need to be deceived. They stood at the pinnacle of power. They were the ones charged with the task of bringing about heaven on earth. They were the ones that supposedly knew how to make this happen so as to usher in a new stage in human history. The belief that success was within their hands was essential if they were to maintain their power and control over the lives of others. They needed to believe that their efforts were moving toward the achievement of their goals. They needed to believe that the workers, peasants, intellectuals, and others were solidly behind them. They needed to believe that traditional religion was dying out and that their new secular religion would take its place. They needed to believe that the young fervently embraced their ideology and that this ideology was going to result in great benefits for mankind. Above all, they needed to believe that socialism works.

A situation is created for those most politically connected as socialism is imposed on the populace. This situation enables them to believe their own deception. The special privilege that they enjoy plays the primary role that enables these rulers to believe their own lies. Throughout the world advocates and practitioners of socialism enjoy the best of everything. They are typically rewarded with the ability to purchase the nicest cars, eat the choicest foods at the finest restaurants, vacation at the best resorts, and travel around the world in first class style. This was as true in the former Soviet Union as it is today in the United States. Such privileges insulate the rulers from the rest of society. In America today, our rulers frequently refer to the main of the nation as "fly-over country." They jet from coast to coast and socialize only with those close to the political reins of power. As such, they look down on ordinary people as being inferior since they live their own lives out in a contrived environment isolated from the rest of society. As a result, they fail to see that they are living their lives as mere parasites on others. Given this situation, they come to actually believe that they are serving humanity as they impose their oppressive socialist policies on others.

In addition to the close circles they keep, they enlist a willing media who are forever hoping to be fellow travelers on the road to the future and, hence, to draw near to special privilege. They become eager participants in spreading the propaganda that socialism is working. No matter what economic disasters result, no matter how shoddy the so-called goods they produce become, the general media seems increasingly willing to promote the idea that all is well with the socialist experimentation. They rely on statistical data that is typically twisted beyond all reason to make the case. Indeed, all who wish to be deceived can be deceived.

The socialist tradition of using statistical data to put a happy face on a lousy economy is alive and well today in the United States. Central planners feel the need to assure citizens that they have everything well under control and that the economy is being wisely directed for the benefit of all.

Consider the issue of the central bank's "management" of interest rates in the United States. What are interest rates going to do? Many wonder, and look to the Federal Reserve for guidance. Surely the central bank should know what the future holds. After all, the media regularly tells us that the Fed "sets" interest rates, and rates will remain low as long as the Fed wants them that way.

The Fed is happy to reinforce the idea that it wisely directs interest rates for the greater good. Consider Fed Chair Janet Yellen's comments at a press conference:

> The Committee [Fed's Open Market Committee] is confident that it has the tools it needs to raise short-term interest rates when it becomes appropriate to do so and to control the level of short-term interest rates thereafter, even though the Federal Reserve will continue to have a very large balance sheet for some time.[16]

Of course, free-market advocates object to the Fed's intervention in lending markets because it distorts interest rates. They argue that economic inefficiencies result from central bank intrusion. They are suspicious that in the long run the Fed cannot simply command interest rates. Rates are essentially a reflection of the preferences of market participants. In an unhindered market they would settle at market clearing rates. Therefore, manipulating rates simply distorts and disrupts free trade.

However, it must be admitted that in the near term there are *some* interest rates the Fed can affect. Take for example the federal funds rate. Following the financial crisis of 2008 the Fed set its target for the federal funds rate in the range of 0 percent to 0.25 percent. And at the time of this writing the Fed funds rate was holding steady at 0.09 percent, near the middle of the Fed's target range.

Those observers who are prone to be deceived might be tempted to congratulate the Fed on its remarkable success at such precise managing of the federal funds rate. But let's not get carried away. Successfully directing the federal funds rate is not much of an accomplishment when one considers what the interest rate is.

Historically the federal funds rate was the interest rate one commercial bank would charge another on a short-term loan of reserves. As such, it was an interest rate determined by voluntary trade between private banks. And as a voluntary agreed upon rate it is very difficult for it to be precisely controlled by a central bank.

All that changed after 2008. Afterwards the Federal Reserve was, and currently is, paying commercial banks 0.25 percent for holding reserves. So if a bank can now earn 0.25 percent for simply sitting on cash, why would it ever extend a loan to another bank at the lower federal funds rate of 0.09 percent? The answer is that they would not. The lending that occurs at the official federal funds rate is largely made by Government Sponsored Entities (Fannie Mae, Freddie Mac, etc.) instead of private commercial banks. This is not much of a free market rate, and it is not surprising that the Fed can successfully manipulate the rate through persuasion. Nevertheless, given the underlying economic realities it is inevitable that this policy will eventually cause all sorts of bad things to happen and some are likely to be quite severe.

The financial industry is not the only area where the U.S. government and the media wish to deceive folks. Consider the health of the labor market as another example. Socialists want people to believe that the government is able to skillfully stimulate the economy so that there is an abundance of good, high-paying jobs. And the statistics they use to report the health of the labor market can be very deceptive.

As of August 2014 the U.S. unemployment rate stood at 6.1 percent.[17] The government and the media trumpeted the economic prosperity that was created through the government's supposedly "excellent" management of the economy.

Receiving less attention has been the declining labor force participation rate, which stood at 62.8 percent—the lowest mark recorded in the past 30 years.[18] How are the falling unemployment rate and labor force participation rate related? To answer this question it is useful to examine what it means to be in the labor force, and also what it means to be unemployed. According to the definitions used by the government's Bureau of Labor Statistics, to be in the labor force somebody must either be employed or unemployed. This seems straightforward, but we also need to understand that being "unemployed" does not simply mean not having a job. To be considered "unemployed" a person must not only be out of work, but also must be *willing* and able to work. A person is not counted as being in the labor force or as being unemployed if he decides he no longer has any desire to find a job. As a result, when a person without a job decides he is no longer interested in looking for work, then both the labor force participation rate and the unemployment rate will simultaneously fall.

One explanation for the drop in labor force participation is that job-seekers became discouraged, and therefore simply quit looking for work. But there is another, even greater force at work. In the case of young adults, the decline in labor force participation is very sharp. This is most likely a consequence of an increase in the number of students attending college—a full-time student is not part of the labor force if he/she is not interested in working while going to school.

Not coincidently, at the same time young people are exiting the labor force in droves the amount of student loan debt has skyrocketed. Student loan debt is increasingly owed to the federal government, as private lenders are unable to compete with the attractive loan repayment plans offered by Uncle Sam. In fact, the U.S. Department of Education encourages students to eschew private lenders while promoting their own taxpayer-financed loans instead. The Department of Education's website touts that, "when it comes to paying for college, career school, or graduate school, federal student loans offer several advantages over private student loans."[19] The Department of Education lists many of the benefits of federal student loans when compared to private loans. For example, it notes that private loans may require a credit check, whereas "you don't need to get a credit check for most federal student loans." Another so-called advantage of federal loans is that, "you may be eligible to have some portion of your loans forgiven if you work in public service. Learn about our loan forgiveness programs." (Read, don't worry too much about whether or not you can pay back the loan—taxpayers have you covered).

Is it any wonder why the labor force participation rate, and also the unemployment rate, fell in this environment? The U.S. government is terrific at finding ways to encourage people to avoid productive employment. Going to school through student loans, which may never have to be repaid, is a big deterrent to entering the labor force. Of course, there are numerous other ways the government discourages people from entering the labor force, and our purpose here is not to provide an exhaustive list. Rather we are demonstrating how statistics are misused to create a deceptive view of economic prosperity.

Of course, people are not all so easily deceived. According to a recent survey, nearly 50 percent of Americans believe the U.S. economy remains in a recession, despite all the glowing statistical reports coming out of the government.[20]

Whether or not people are actually deceived by the deceptions is somewhat beside the point. The point is that reality becomes sufficiently distorted so that it is more and more difficult to determine what is real and what is not. When the truth is so distorted and obscured that people find it difficult to discover what it is, people may believe whatever they wish to believe. The purpose of the deception is adequately achieved when those who need to believe are enabled to do so.

Looking back in time to the former Soviet Union, the communists went to great lengths to build façade after façade to assist everyone to believe that their socialism was the wave of the future. Unfortunately for them, one of the results of widespread deception was an equally widespread cynicism. The Soviet engineers in our opening story attest to this result. They simply could not believe that such a large number of automobiles could have been assembled in one place except for the purpose of deceiving and impressing them. Of course, that same doubt meant that they did not believe the façades of the communists in their own country either. Nevertheless, in public everyone pretended to believe even though in private they knew the truth.

Such pretense undoubtedly degraded them, but degraded men are essential to corrupt systems. That the Soviet system was corrupt should not be doubted. Neither should it be doubted that political corruption runs rampant wherever the idea has gained ground.

Behind all of this was a grim and brutal reality. It was the reality of fear and terror. The power wielded by the Soviet rulers could only be maintained by fear and the exercise of terror. People who are unafraid of death cannot be herded so easily along the socialist way. In order to promote the fear of death, the communists used terror. As laws multiplied and family members were heralded as heroes for turning in perpetrators, people had no place in which to feel shielded from government intrusion. People lived in constant fear that the secret police might show up in the night to haul them off on some trumped up charges. Such charges could easily result in the person being shipped off to some slave labor camp or worse. As a result, pretense and cynicism reigned supreme.

In America today political corruption is rampant and the deceptions being created by the political class in Washington D.C. bear a remarkable resemblance to those of the former Soviet Empire. As a result, trust of elected officials is at an all time low and closing in on zero. Yet we continue merrily down the evolutionary road to socialism believing the outcome will be different here.

Four

The Massive State
and the Impotent Populace

The state is the great fictitious entity by which everyone seeks to live at the expense of everyone else.
— Frédéric Bastiat, "The State"[21]

The idea that has the world in its grip invariably promotes the growth of government, which reduces the freedom of the individual. Whether socialism is pursued by revolutionary means or evolutionary means makes little difference. In either case the aim is to increase government's control over people. Moreover, the idea itself intends that very outcome. It intends to subjugate the individual to the government's control and to make him a dependent. Further, dependency is achieved by way of coercion, which spreads fear among the citizenry.

One of the chief problems with the expansion of state power is that it undercuts the productive efforts of people. As the state gains control over more and more of the economy, less and less is actually produced. Furthermore, that which is produced is of poorer and poorer quality. For example, according to many erroneous accounts, in its heyday the Soviet Union was one of the leading industrial nations of the world. In actuality its main export was communist ideology. A country that can only dispose of its shoddy merchandise by erecting barriers to keep other goods out and prevent its inhabitants from going elsewhere to shop should not have been styled a leading industrial nation. Indeed, in hindsight the Soviet Union collapsed because of its economic ineptitude. That nation was little more than a jailor nation. The lesson of this collapse should serve notice to the world, which seems bent on going down the same path. Americans of all people should realize the folly of this path, yet the march toward socialism continues apace here.

The delusions of socialists arise from Marxian and communist ideology. Karl Marx had the delusion that he had discovered the secret of history. His notion about the inevitable triumph of the proletariat is no more scientific than the belief that the position of the planets controls our destiny. Yet his ideology provided the foundation for modern rulers and would-be rulers to embrace the belief that the way to the future was through using the force of government to bring about paradise on earth. That belief is nothing more than a grand lie.

Are socialists simply insane? After all, it has often been said that insanity is continuing to do the same thing today that failed to achieve the desired result yesterday. However, there is a crucial difference between the insane person and the person committed to ideology. The insane person suffers from his own action while the ideologist imposes suffering on others. Neither Marx nor any socialist ruler has suffered significantly from imposing his plans on others. That is, with the exception when he might be overthrown and executed. But as long as he maintains his power he inflicts hardship on the populace while reaping personal rewards.

The perverse effects of the delusions of socialists are accounted for by the assumptions and presumptions of the ideology. Karl Marx had what may be best described as a criminal mind. Not the mind of a petty thief, of course. Not even the mind of those who are ordinarily thought of as directing organized crime. He had a cosmic criminal mind.

The crime that Marx contemplated was theft, the theft of all property used in the production and distribution of goods. While Marx advocated the method of revolution to carry out this theft, it is hardly different under the rule of democratic socialists who aim at the same end by a fifty-one percent vote. Those who are enlisted as cohorts in stealing the fruits of the labor or others are enticed by the prospect of enjoying the government's largess. In this sense, Marxism and socialism are merely parallel plans for carrying out robbery. But Marx added two dimensions to this crime that other thieves do not ordinarily consider. First, he declared that this act of universal robbery was inevitable. Second, he conceived an ideology that supposedly justified the thievery. Put simply, he proposed theft without guilt. He wove the whole thing together into a framework of an anti-religious religion.

The universal plunder that Marx prescribed was, of course, to be only a prelude to a supposedly universal justice, peace, harmony, well-being, and freedom. Man was to be emancipated from all the constraints that kept his true nature from emerging. He was to be transformed, following upon the transformation of the economy, and a new society would emerge. The eventual end would justify the means, though Marx believed the plunder was justified as well. Marx gave no specific details as to what this new society or the new man would be like. Presumably they would emerge naturally once the expropriation was complete and the means of production were in the hands of the "workers."

If theft can be justified, then all other crimes are justified as well. Torture, slavery, extortion, compulsion, murder, fraud, threats, assault, and every species of restraint can be done. If stealing is justified, nay, required, then all resistance to theft must be met with whatever force is necessary to overcome it. The force to overcome resistance to the robbery must be greater than all the energy men may use to cling to their possessions.

It is not simply that man has an affinity for property, though he has; it is even more the case that property has an affinity for man, so to speak. To put it more directly, property must be owned before it realizes its potential as property. Property without ownership is an abstraction, an abstraction waiting for an owner to appear and give it character and fulfillment. To call it public property is only an attempt to obfuscate ownership. There is still someone who decides how it is to be used. To divest man of this relationship and prevent him from forming it runs counter to the natural, metaphysical chemistry between man and property. If it was justified, then every imaginable assault upon man is justified, even his murder.

Universalized theft, or nationalized theft, as it has been practiced thus far, requires universalized force. This accounts for the rise of massive state governments in the various nations around the world. Whether it was the former Soviet Union, or China, or the rapidly increasing size of the U.S. federal government, each is the result of the spread of the idea that has the world in its grip. The swell in the size of governments has its roots in the nature of property as well. Property requires attention if it is to be productive. Divesting individuals of private property does not remove this requirement. Instead, it aggravates it. The property that governments take over must be managed somehow. As governments take over property there is an increasing need of bureaucracy and bureaucrats aimed at managing what has been stolen.

There are necessary delusions that must be believed if this ideology is to be imposed. They are the delusions of the criminal mind writ large. Theft is a crime; so are all the acts done in support of it. Marx conceived the most monstrous crime imaginable. The various governmental rulers of the world, whether they are of the revolutionary or evolutionary variety, have been the ones carrying out the crime and thus spreading the idea worldwide. It was and is necessary that they do not think of themselves as criminals. Yet that is what they are. To avoid that realization the notion that theft is a crime must be held to be invalid. The moral code that prohibits theft must be denied. The cultural heritage that bolsters property and private rights must be negated and set aside. The age-old conceptions of human nature must be put to naught. All that is left is human will, the will to believe, and the force that resides in the government's monopoly of power. The more closely the ideology is fulfilled, the more impotent the populace. The more massive the state, the more helpless the people become.

Therein lies the dilemma with all forms of socialism no matter the degree to which it is practiced. To succeed, socialist economies must engage the efforts, wills, energies, and initiative of all the people in them. But these are held in check by the massive state, by the ever increasing and ubiquitous police, by the swollen bureaucracy, and by the forced commitment to the ideology. These necessary elements of socialism destroy the abilities of the people to act effectively. The only way for the people to become more effective is to reduce the size of the state and to increase the individual freedom of the people. Every step in that direction is in direct opposition to the ideology of socialism itself. This dilemma cannot be resolved. It is inherent to the very nature of socialism in all its varieties.

In an effort to ignore this dilemma, socialists believe that it is possible to simply change human nature. They mistakenly think that they can eradicate the individual's pursuit of self-interest. A moment's contemplation of the condition in which we find ourselves living in this world should be sufficient to discover that any action we engage in is a self-interested action since only the individual self can act. Moreover, human consciousness is such that only the individual is aware of his needs and wants and what priorities he has. To live in this world it is necessary for the individual to take care of his own immediate needs. We must look for oncoming traffic before crossing streets. We must be careful not to eat things that might harm us as well as to eat a sufficient amount of those things that will sustain us. The various issues of daily life require so much human action of the self-interested variety that it will do little good to suppose that such behavior can be dispensed with.

A second misconception of socialists is that removing the cultural supports of the individual will root out self-interest and lead to greater civility. On the contrary, cultural supports of the individual provide an adequate framework that limits, restrains, and civilizes his self-interested actions. Given such cultural supports, people tend to limit their own actions in the pursuit of their self-interest. Good manners require us to take our places in line and to defer to others on many occasions simply because it is in our best interest to do so. We begin to recognize and respect the equal rights of others because we know our own rights and want them to be respected. We know that living in peace and harmony with others is in our self-interest and, therefore, in pursuing our interest we naturally defer to others when it is appropriate to do so. This can often be seen most cohesively in a well-functioning family. It is often necessary in families for some member or members of it to act in apparently selfless ways for the greater good of the family. But these are simply the self-interested choices of the actors and what they value at the moment they choose.

One of the great missions of culture and civilization is to provide a peaceful and harmonious framework within which the individual can seek his own interests constructively. To destroy the culture because it supports the individual will not alter the individual's pursuit of self-interest. It will only remove the restraints on it. The reason for this should be clear. Our pursuit of self-interest is not culturally induced. It arises from our nature and the world that we inhabit. Socialism of all forms pits itself not only against culture, but against human nature as well.

A third delusion of socialists is that government force can be used to transform human nature. So far as we know, human nature cannot be changed by threat of force. While it is true that human behavior can be altered by the threat of punishment, it is not at all clear that force is the best means of bringing out the best efforts of the individual. While punishment might effectively limit wrongdoing, it is the weakest means of producing rightdoing. Rightdoing proceeds from and engages the best efforts or the wills of individuals. Force can produce a modicum of obedience, but it will not engage the greater part of the ingenuity and creativity of the person being coerced.

An early enthusiast of the former Soviet Union once remarked, "I have seen the future, and it works." However, those who examined the course of that Union over a longer period of time had a better statement that captured the reality of it. They scoffed, "I have seen the future of Communism, and not even the plumbing works." Perhaps this joke was more of a half-truth than the whole truth. There were, of course, some toilets that worked at least some of the time. Nevertheless, it is clear that the general quality of all construction projects in the Soviet Union was poor. Anyone who visited the remains of that Union shortly after its collapse can attest to this reality.

The economic failure of the Soviet Union also provides evidence of the vacuous nature of macroeconomics. Aggregated data tell us little about the economic efficacy of a nation's GDP. As the Union plunged toward economic collapse, there were many who touted the economic success of the USSR based upon the trend of its increasing GDP. They even went so far as to predict that it would eventually overtake that of the U.S. The truth, however, was quite the opposite. There is no comparison between goods produced by decree and those produced to supply wants registered in the market. Goods produced by decree are qualitatively inferior; they are orphans in the market place, seeking some kindhearted soul who will adopt them. Macroeconomics can only deal with them by declaring them equal to all other goods so that they can be reduced to statistics. Since they are not, the result can only be a deception. This reveals an unfortunate truth about macroeconomics. Namely, that it is a pseudo-science where the greatest truth that we are able to discover is that statistics can be used to deceive. Indeed, if you torture the data long enough, you can make them confess to most anything.

The economic failures of the former Soviet economy are most telling when one realizes that their central planners inherited one of the most productive grain-producing areas of the world and succeeded in so destroying its output that Russia eventually had to import such products to sustain its populace. Its industrial production was hardly better. In fact, a multi-volume encyclopedia on how not to produce goods and services could be compiled from the Soviet experience. The "successful" plant manager in that environment aimed at having the lowest possible mandated quota and stockpiling large inventories of parts so that he might easily achieve turning out a sufficient quantity of shoddy goods to exceed his quota.

Fear of failing to achieve the central planners' mandates drove the whole system. That fear is perhaps best captured in what one Soviet inspector observed:

> As inspector I once arrived at a plant which was supposed to have delivered mining machines, but did not do so. When I entered the plant premises, I saw that machines were piled up all over the place, but they were unfinished. I asked what was going on. The director gave evasive answers. Finally, when the big crowd surrounding us had disappeared, he called me into his office.[22]

There, the story came out. It seems that the specifications for the machines called for them to be painted with red oil-resistant varnish. But the only red varnish the plant possessed was not oil-resistant. The manager did have green oil-resistant varnish, but was afraid to use it since that would have violated the instructions. The inspector knew the need for the machines and that it made little difference whether they were painted red or green, but he too feared a prison sentence should he change the authorization. As a result, he cabled the central planners in Moscow hoping for a quick decision. Apparently, the planners in Moscow did not want to make the decision either as it took an incredibly long time to hear back from them. Finally, the approval to use green paint came in. Nevertheless, the inspector made a copy of the cable and put it in his pocket for the rest of his life just in case someone might call him on the carpet for altering the specifications.

Such inefficiencies were rampant throughout the Soviet economy. It was not too long ago that Americans would have laughed at the idea that this would happen. However, these same inefficiencies are increasingly present in the U.S. economy as the rules and regulations imposed by the various federal government agencies multiply exponentially. Whole new departments of compliance consume ever-larger portions of the budget in American industry and add substantial costs to production. More and more people fear the reprisals of government bureaucrats. One may never know when he might be hauled into a court of law for violating some federal regulation that has the weight of federal law. As a result, entrepreneurial efforts at the small business level grind to a halt leading to economic stagnation.

The greatest failures of establishing massive socialist governments are not economic. The greatest failures are social and spiritual. Some modicum of production continues when central planning is the chief method of economic control. However, *which* products to be produced are determined by those possessing the political power. Their preferences trump those of the general populace. Innovation and creativity are stifled. The result is that there is a horrendous cost in the lives of the people. The truth is that the greater the government's control, the greater the suffering and deprivation of the people, and the greater the wasted natural resources of the nation. Perhaps the best example of this in our world today is the nation of North Korea. An utterly thuggish dictator rules it and he has conscripted almost the entire productive effort of the nation to his personal whims. As a result, the people are literally starving to death and often attempt to make death-defying escapes for the relatively greater freedom of China.

The idea that has the world in its grip has launched what amounts to an alien assault upon people generally. The assault upon humanity is massive indeed. It attacks the individual's spirit, his individuality, his religion, and his family. That force is attacking society itself. The assault has been carried out by the assembled power of an increasingly totalitarian state. It has been carried out by all the devices conceivable to a criminal mind: brutal murder, torture, propaganda, threats, exile, mass starvation, and terror. While the intensity of these devices depends on the current scale and imposition of the idea, they are nevertheless true to some degree throughout the world. A gigantic effort has been made to wipe out the heritage of the people and to destroy the ancient bonds of community. The goal is to break the people under the wheel of the state. Anyone who is at all concerned with the well-being of his fellow man should view this situation with sorrow and should vigorously oppose the continued spread of the idea.

While the intensity of the imposition of the idea has abated to a degree in some parts of the world, that has not come about apart from the infliction of numerous wounds, which has left ugly scars. Surely, it has broken many of the bonds of community. The family has been sorely tried by the heavy-handed state. In the former Soviet Union informing on one another, even by close family members, became commonplace. This surely broke the bonds of trust within the family structure. Even in its milder forms of evolutionary socialism, the rates of divorce have increased. As more and more families rely upon the incomes of both husband and wife to sustain a particular lifestyle, the levels of stress increase as well. In addition, institutional religion has increasingly been made to be subservient to the state. As the idea becomes more pervasive, society increasingly loses control over her institutions. Propaganda takes its toll upon the mental development of the citizenry who increasingly become ill-informed. Fear of retribution tends to drive frank conversations into the nooks and crannies.

Despite the onslaught of government power and force, human nature survives. Nearing its total collapse, Russian farmers vigorously pursued their own self-interest by producing more product on their small private plots of land than was produced on vast amounts of corporate farm land. People there were ever alert to hear what might be available in the stores and would often scurry out to stand in long lines in the hope of securing some of the merchandise. Most notably, the self-interest of the Party members was always on display as they shopped in specialty stores for products that were not available to the masses. The truth is that people generally have no interest in committing suicide, which is what the abandonment of self-interest entails. While governments may hamper and hinder people in countless ways with a vast web of rules and regulations, people will still pursue their self-interest as certainly as they pursued alcoholic beverages during Prohibition in America.

In the former Soviet Union the maintenance of self-interest did not come without a cost. The wound was nowhere deeper and the scars nowhere uglier than what was left of society in the Soviet Union. We live our lives out in a variety of spheres. Where people are moderately free, there are several realms: the realm of government, the realm of society, and the realm of the individual that is personal and private. These are not exclusive spheres; they are rather complementary, interdependent, and interacting realms. When the idea gains ground the spheres of real society recede as government gains ground.

Society encompasses that realm of social relationships that are largely voluntary, the realm of manners, customs, traditions, morality, and ways by which individuals live fruitfully and peacefully with one another. The cultural heritage is activated and carried on largely by society. It is the arena of influence and persuasion rather than force. What the Soviet Union did was to attempt to destroy this realm of human interaction. In doing so its actual aim was to destroy the trust, confidence and general goodwill upon which all societies depend. Human freedom along with trust, confidence and goodwill can hardly survive in a world where children inform on their parents, or neighbors upon neighbors, or husbands upon wives. Such informing was fostered and encouraged. It was even required. Throughout the Union there was surveillance, hidden microphones, wire taps, listening devices, and the creation of extensive dossiers on the populace. Those in America today should be very suspicious of the same sort of behavior being exercised by the police and other government officials since this kind of activity goes hand-in-hand with the idea that has the world in its grip.

For people and societies to flourish, voluntary institutions are necessary. Churches, clubs, private associations, markets, hospitals and a whole host of other such institutions provide the fabric among people that builds such things as trust, confidence, and goodwill. When these are either stripped away by government or brought under the thumb of government control, society itself is severely damaged. The lines of communication on which society depends are clogged by a massive state.

When the state consolidates its power and control, two developments in society take place. One is a crudeness of relationships in general. Government clerks are usually rude and harsh of manner. Any visit to one's local department of motor vehicles provides sufficient evidence that this is true. When employment in such governmental activities becomes pervasive this spills over into the general relationships of life. As Hedrick Smith observed regarding the general tenor of Soviet behavior, the Russian manner came across in "public as coarse indifference, passive fatalism, and pushy discourtesy. Western visitors have commented on the glum, shuttered faces of Russian street crowds, and the brusque, negative surliness of service people."[23] If a visitor might offer a friendly hello to a passing Russian citizen, the only response would have been a vacant stare.

This coarseness of social relations evinces itself in yet another way—in busybodiness, which has no doubt been promoted by the spread of the idea. Once again, an example from the former Soviet Union provides evidence of this. Leona Schechter, who once spent several years in Moscow during the communist reign, told a story about taking her child to school on a cold winter day. She had neglected to dress herself warmly against the cold. Just as she was about to enter the school she was accosted by a woman who began to scold her for not being better dressed. To escape the situation she told the woman that she did not want her child to be late and was briefly released from being reprimanded. However, upon leaving the building the same woman was waiting to pick up on haranguing her. She said it was her socialist duty to do so.[24] Socialist duty it might have been, but sociable it was not.

The other development is that society, such as it can be, must be rebuilt in tightly knit private circles. Friends gathered in kitchens or other private settings where they could be reasonably safe from the prying eyes of informers and the ever-ubiquitous police. Only then could spontaneous and free communication take place. Such small groups offered people the human need to socialize with others. As a general rule, these social groups tend to expand in size and openness when the idea is on the retreat in a nation and to become smaller when government oppression is on the rise.

When considering the rise of the massive state, which inhibits human action, it should once again be pointed out that the idea is an anti-religious religion. That is, it must seek to root out and destroy the practice of religion itself. But this was perhaps the most dramatic failure of Soviet Communism. To be sure it aimed to destroy the Christian religion as it was practiced in its realm. Decades of atheistic propaganda, the widespread closing of churches, the denial of general access to the means of study, worship, and religious training failed to accomplish the sought after result. Of course, the assault on religion did do great damage. While it did not destroy Christianity, it did destroy the social and communal benefits of its practice. It drove the practice of Christianity underground thus depriving public life of the redeeming values of its admonitions to love one's neighbor as one's self. In truth, whether the idea is promoted in its revolutionary or evolutionary form, all secularists must attack traditional religious convictions. It is as true in America as it was in the Soviet Union.

Though the Soviets succeeded in building a massive state, Soviet Communism failed. It failed to provide people with goods and services economically and competitively. It failed to root out self-interest. It failed to significantly alter human nature. It failed to build a new society. And, it failed to crush religion. Given the complete and utter failure of the idea in its most aggressive form one is left to wonder why there are those who still advocate for it and pursue it in its evolutionary form. It is a fool's errand.

Five

Coercing Our Way to Paradise

> In fact, if law were restricted to protecting all persons, all liberties, and all properties; if law were nothing more than the organized combination of the individual's right to self-defense; if law were the obstacle, the check, the punisher of all oppression and plunder—is it likely that we citizens would then argue much about the extent of the franchise?
> — Frédéric Bastiat, *The Law*[25]

As was discussed earlier, the practical spread of the idea that has the world in its grip has come in two forms: revolutionary and evolutionary socialism. To get a better understanding of how the idea has actually come to dominate popular opinion and then to be imposed around the world we need to examine a few examples of each form. In its revolutionary form we have seen the idea promoted in Russia, Germany, China, Cambodia, North Korea, and many other countries in Asia, Africa, Central and South America. The other nations of the world have largely gone down the path of evolutionary socialism. In fact, most of the world remains on this path including Western Europe, the countries that emerged from the former Soviet Union, Canada, The United States, Australia, New Zealand, and the non-revolutionary countries of Asia, Africa, Central and South America. Even revolutionary China has in recent years backed off the revolutionary approach in favor of what is tantamount to a more evolutionary path to control. Given the near universal spread of the idea it is worthwhile to consider briefly a few examples of each form.

The Revolutionary Way

In practice revolutionary socialism begins either with the use of force or with an election that is promptly followed by the consolidation of power and the imposition of the idea by force. Either way, guns are quickly employed to force people to do what the proponents conceive of as being the way to the common good to achieve paradise on earth. In addition, every regime practicing the revolutionary form of socialism appears to be capricious as long as we use traditional terminology to discuss their behavior. Whether we are discussing Stalin, Mao, Castro, or Hitler, all seem to be driven by some sort of perverse sickness. But once it is realized that each was fundamentally tied to socialist ideology, their individual abuses of power become easily recognizable as flowing from the idea that has the world in its grip. Despite whatever peculiarities each practiced, at the core they all used secrecy, terror, purges, violence, and fear to accomplish their socialistic aims. Perhaps the best example of the forced overthrow of the existing order took place in Russia with the Bolshevik revolution and the best example of how an election was quickly turned to the revolution is what took place in Germany when the Nazis came to power there.

First, consider the Bolshevik revolution. It followed on the heels of the dissolving power and authority of the Russian Czar. Political conflict in March of 1917 in the city of St. Petersburg (called Petrograd at the time) had resulted in a situation that forced Nicholas II to abdicate his throne. This event set the stage for the eventual rise of the communist revolution later that year since it threw into doubt what governmental order would replace the existing one. Thus, it was the dissolution of the traditional governmental structures that opened the door for the revolutionaries.

After Nicholas abdicated the throne, a provisional government was set up. At the time the Bolsheviks were a minority party vying with other parties to influence the direction of the nation. How then were they able to seize power? The answer can be reduced to a single word—Violence. Led by Vladimir Lenin they launched their revolution in November 1917 (it was October based on the calendar in use in Russia at the time) by taking over the Winter Palace where the provisional government was in session. In fear for their lives, the officials quickly gave their power over to the Bolsheviks. Over the course of the next several months they continued to use violence or the threat of it to consolidate their control over the entire country. To insure their power they then executed Nicholas and his entire family in July 1918.

According to Marxian theory, Russia was not even close to being ripe for a communist revolution. After all, it was a backward country. The populace was mostly rural and engaged in farming rather than in industrial enterprises. While the needs of supporting the military activities of WWI had resulted in some expansion of industrial activities, these remained small in comparison to what most people did. The situation did not fit into the Marxian explanation of the need for revolution. Nevertheless, Lenin was enthralled by Marxism and employed several strategies to justify his revolutionary efforts. By offering up this theoretical justification Lenin opened the door for the revolution to spread to other backward countries.

Once power was securely in their hands, the Bolsheviks then turned to implementing the details of the revolution. They seized control over property and began an assault on the family and religion. In one pamphlet, Alexandra Kollontai had this to say:

> The family ceases to be necessary. It is not necessary to the state because domestic economy is no longer advantageous to the state, it needlessly distracts women workers from more useful productive labour. It is not necessary to members of the family themselves because the other task of the family—the bringing up of children—is gradually taken over by society.[26]

While Lenin did not go so far, he did require civil registration for marriage and made religious ceremonies of no account by law. Both sexes were declared equal and abortion was legalized in 1920. In addition to efforts to undercut family ties, the communists seized Church property and banned any religious practices from the schools. Moreover, there was widespread persecution of those who were religiously inclined.

By 1921, Russia was in virtual ruins. Instead of the bright utopian future that had been promised, there was only devastation. Industrial production was only thirteen percent of what it had been prior to World War I. In comparison to the seventy-four million tons of grain harvested in 1916, 1919's harvest stood at thirty million tons. Because of the rapid increase in the supply of money by the Bolsheviks, its value had dropped precipitously. Famine was everywhere. The population of St. Petersburg had dropped from 2,416,000 to 722,000 and that of Moscow from 2 million to 800,000. The situation was desperate. It was so bad that Lenin had to back off of the revolution and restore at least some individual freedom so that some people could survive. As a result, things did improve somewhat.

Nevertheless, terror became the substitute for law in Russia. Terror is as essential to communism as oxygen is to fire. It is simply in its nature. Marx argued that when private property is abolished the state would wither away. But that assumption was a gross error. Far from withering away, the state became all encompassing. It sought to occupy every nook and cranny of everyone's life. What withers away under communism is not the state, but law, liberty, private rights, and justice. While Marx thought that the law was the means by which some men oppress other men, the truth is that there is a necessity of decorum among men, a rule of order to secure our relationships with one another. If Marxian experimentation teaches us anything, it is that law is neither essential to nor derived from the power of the state. Instead, law is an impediment to the exercise of governmental power. Governments operate by using force and the state assumes a monopoly of that force within its jurisdiction. What the law does is to regulate and limit the use of force by government. Law is no more necessary to government than handcuffs are to a boxer.

Governmental rule in the former Soviet Union was one of the most oppressive and tyrannical known in human history. It reached its height of oppression under Joseph Stalin, though tyranny prevailed throughout the communist domination of the people. In practice communism is *rule by gangsters*. The rulers seek their legitimacy by their appeal to Marxist ideology. Nevertheless, gangsters are what they were in the Soviet Union and what they are wherever communism is still practiced. It is not simply that communists seize power by force and that they conspire with one another to consolidate their power. They do, of course, do both things. But what makes them gangsters is that they are thieves.

In truth, the Soviet Union was at bottom a lawless nation. To be sure there were plenty of rules and regulations, but these were a façade.

The government ruled over the people using terror. The extent of terror depended solely upon the particular ruler. The need for terror was necessitated by communism.

The history of the Soviet Union can be divided into episodes according to the degree, extent, and quality of terror by which it was ruled. The first episode was that of War Communism from 1918 into 1921. It was a period of extensive terror and draconian rule. The economic disaster of this episode led to that of the New Economic Policy (NEP), which lasted from 1921 to 1928. During this time terror abated somewhat as people were allowed to engage in a variety of private economic activities. The economy recovered some during this episode. However, it was followed by the reign of Joseph Stalin who ruled from 1928 to 1953. The most extensive and intensive terror of the Soviet era occurred during this time period. While no one knows exactly, official Russian documents provide evidence that nearly three million were killed under his regime. That number does not account for the many other victims who died early deaths in slave labor camps or those starving to death during periods of famine. Stalin was followed by Khrushchev, who was not as heavy-handed. He in turn was followed by Brezhnev, who stepped up the terror and activities of the secret police. To be sure, all used the secret police as a tool to keep the people in line and to consolidate their power and control.

To better understand life in the Soviet Union throughout these episodes it is useful to consider the process by which terror was employed. The purpose of terror was to produce conformity among the people. While it was never regularized, for no one could predict when it would be employed, there was a pattern to it. It would begin when someone was arrested by the secret police and taken in for questioning. This would occur at a local prison where the person would be interrogated for extended periods of time. The interrogation itself was designed to bring the maximum amount of psychological and physical pressure on the person. The prisoner was essentially broken down to the point that a confession to some crime could be obtained. Once a confession was secured, the prisoner would be sentenced. The sentence could range from the death penalty to forced labor in a gulag. The whole process was arbitrary and there was no appeal for actual facts. Rather, the only thing that the authorities were interested in was securing a satisfactory confession. In such an environment, most people simply hope to make it through life unseen.

The final episode of the Soviet Union occurred under the reign of Gorbachev. The economy had become so poor that he instituted policies supposedly offering new freedoms to the people. But these were too little and too late. He was as much a communist as his predecessors and the Soviet Union crumbled around him coming to final end in 1991. The conditions of life in the countries emerging from this breakup have varied depending upon the degree to which they have sufficiently restored the economic freedom of the people in them and secured their property with some semblance of a working rule of law.

The revolutionary path to utopia does not have to start with guns though. In some cases it begins with an election that is quickly followed by using guns to seize near total control over a country. This is what happened in Germany in the 1930s. In the presence of his prospective cabinet and President Hindenburg of the Weimar Republic, Adolf Hitler was sworn in as German Chancellor on January 30, 1933. In his oath of office he swore to uphold the nation's constitution and discharge the duties of his office according to the nation's legal code. Yet, within months of this ceremony about the only relic of the Weimar Republic that remained was President Hindenburg and he did not survive long thereafter. A Nazi revolution had taken place. It was accomplished by the suppression of liberty, the confiscation of property, the enslavement of opponents in concentration camps, and the persecution of people generally with terror and violence.

"You will know them by their fruits,"[27] Scripture says. By contrast, ideologists contend that by their *intentions* you must distinguish among them. It is crucial to understand this mode of thinking as it is practiced, particularly by socialist ideologues. The idea that has the world in its grip gains adherents, spreads, and tightens its hold because of the alleged good intentions of its believers. The results of the idea are everywhere destructive. The degree of the destruction depends mainly on the extent of the application. But this is obscured as much as possible behind a smokescreen of good intentions.

If the methods of Adolf Hitler in Nazi Germany are compared to those of Joseph Stalin, it can be shown that their differences are insignificant alongside their similarities. It amounts to the difference of disposing of unwanted people by a shot in the back of the head or death in a frozen wasteland as was practiced in Russia versus the Nazi's preference for poison gas. Interestingly, most people tend to view the Nazis and the Communists as entirely different species. That the Nazis and the Communists were usually political opponents is true, but there is no reason to conclude from that fact that they belonged to opposite ends of the political spectrum. The rivalry between brothers is often intense which is not something new. Indeed, Cain slew Abel out of his jealousy. The truth is that communism and Nazism were brothers under the skin.

The full name of the Nazi Party was the National Socialist German Workers' Party. While some have attempted to argue that Hitler was not a socialist, he certainly claimed to be one. He was most definitely a collectivist. All of the mass meetings, the raised hand salute in unison, the cries of "Seig Heil," the jack-booted soldiers on parade, and the highly emotional speeches were all intended to provide the populace with a shared experience and a common vision. Nazism was collectivist just as socialism is collectivist. In addition, the kinship is shown by the fact that all forms of collectivism aim to promote the idea that has the world in its grip. Namely, that governmental force can be used to bring about paradise on earth by reshaping human nature. All socialist ideologies, whatever their differences, aim at the same thing. While the perceived ills of society that must be overcome to achieve this result may vary, the mode of operation does not.

According to Hitler, the main ill that Germany faced was the Jews and their intellectual offspring. In his mind Jewish culture, democracy, finance capitalism, and so on had to be destroyed in order to promote Aryan society. To him the Jews were the exploiters of the people just as the capitalists were the exploiters in communism. The German race was to the Nazis what the proletariat was to Communists. Hitler called for the German workers to throw off the oppression of the Jews. Hitler was a revolutionary and he made no secret of it. "National Socialism as a matter of principle," he said, "must lay claim to the right to force its principles on the whole German nation.... It must determine and reorder the life of a people."[28] Hitler aimed to tear down this world to build another one. He promised to replace this world with one that was organically unified.

It is likely that Hitler's stint in prison in the 1920s led him to believe that his revolution could not be undertaken immediately by force.

However, it is also likely that prison did not convert him to acting within the means of legality. Rather, it is most probable that he realized at this time that the political power of the Reichstag could be used for revolutionary means if he could gain control over it. As much as he despised elections, they offered the most likely route to power. Thus he worked tirelessly to build the Nazi Party to seek political power through the ballot box. In 1932 the Nazis became the leading party in the Reichstag and were then able install Hitler as chancellor in 1933.

From this point on the Nazis moved quickly to consolidate their power and control over the country. While they did not directly expropriate private property, the owners could not continue to use it as they saw fit but had to conform to the arbitrary dictates of the Nazi government. Moreover, they did not tolerate any political competition. They used the same tactics used by the Bolsheviks in Russia. Namely, they employed violence and the threat of violence to ensure submission to their rule. For the German people the only choice was either to blend in with the organic whole that the Nazis sought or to flee from Germany. Anyone unable to flee and unwilling to blend in was persecuted. If you were Jewish your only options were to flee or to be persecuted.

The horror of the holocaust leveled upon the Jewish people is well-known. Anyone who has toured through one of the concentration camps can attest to the inhumanity. One such camp was Auschwitz located in Poland, a country that fell under German occupation in 1940. The first Jewish prisoners arrived there shortly after it was opened. Initially, the prisoners were just forced to work as slave labor, but that quickly changed when the Germans began experimenting in various ways. After some prisoners were killed with poison gas, this method of execution expanded rapidly. So much so that the Germans built Birkenau, located just a few miles away from the main Auschwitz camp. Birkenau was essentially designed as a death factory. Trains would enter the facility in the center of the camp. On each side of the tracks were barracks that housed those prisoners who would be put to slave labor. When the trains arrived the prisoners would disembark and then be stripped of all their personal belongings. They were lined up and a "health" officer would make a quick determination as to whether or not a person was fit for work. Those selected for work would be separated from the women, children, the elderly, and those of poor health. People not selected for work would then be marched to the end of the camp. At that end there were two large gas chambers on each side of the tracks. Attached to them were incinerators. The women, children, elderly men, and men of poor health would be stripped naked and forced into the gas chambers to be killed. Afterwards their bodies were incinerated.

The horror of this is unspeakable. The question has often been raised why the Nazis did not meet greater opposition in Germany. Why, it has been asked, didn't the state leaders, political parties, and labor unions mount any real opposition? Why didn't church leaders speak out strongly against Hitler? Why did business leaders so readily go along? Why didn't the army oppose the spread of barbarism and terror? What happened to the voices of journalists, writers, judges, lawyers, artists, and others who are thought to be keepers of civility? Why didn't these people and others raise a storm of opposition to this awful inhumanity? Perhaps the broadest answer to these questions is that Germany was divided and the divisions served as an impediment to action. In addition, on the surface, the Nazis had risen to power by what was thought to be legal means. Thus, while they were violating every rule of lawful government, the fact that they had come to occupy their offices democratically worked against focused opposition to their rule.

What collectivist ideologies attempt to achieve is organic unity of the collective. They see the basic human problem as being associated with some group, class, or race and blame all ills that beset society on them. The Communists blamed the capitalists, imperialists, or whatever, while the Nazis blamed the Jews. Both Nazi and Marxist ideologues sometimes presented their cases very simplistically. For the Marxist it was necessary for the proletariat to seize power and the means of production in order to usher in paradise. For the Nazi it was necessary to suppress and eliminate the Jews. If we are sober in our judgments, we are all aware of our own imperfections and shortcomings. Since society is made up of imperfect people, the notion that paradise on earth can be had is a false vision. Rather than coming to grips with this reality, collectivists attempt to project their guilt upon others and then seek to eliminate them. In the process they debase themselves and become some of the worst devils to walk the face of the earth. This is why mass murder has invariably been associated with the revolutionary way.

The Evolutionary Way

While the evolutionary way to utopia has not been so barbaric or violent, at least not yet, it nevertheless aims at the same destination. The bulk of today's world has been traveling down this path. The main tools gradualists employ to achieve the implementation of the idea by political means are governmental regulations on commerce, the nationalization of key industries, and the redistribution of wealth for the supposed purpose of fostering the general welfare. The ballot box is their chief means to gain power and control. In the political realm they try to minimize any real differences between political parties to give the appearance of greater national unity of purpose even in the presence of competing interests. To examine the practice of gradualism we will look briefly at England, the United States, and Sweden.

A good case can be made that England was the birthplace of evolutionary socialism. This fact is somewhat ironic since England was the leading capitalist country of the nineteenth century. Nevertheless, it was also the safe haven for socialist advocates like Karl Marx who were left free to toil away there. Thus *Das Kapital* was published in England. Shortly after its publication, Eduard Bernstein put forth an evolutionary theory of socialism by making a major revision of Marx's work.

True economic freedom for the general populace has not been a reality for most people in most times. Indeed, the spread of free enterprise in practice is something rather new in human history. It was most fully embraced by the English in the late eighteenth and early nineteenth centuries. The academic works of men like Adam Smith, David Hume, and Jean Baptist Say were embraced by others such as Richard Cobden who led campaigns for overthrowing the vast web of regulations, rules, taxes, and restrictions on enterprise that were essential features of Mercantilism. This resulted in freeing people to engage in various enterprises of their own choosing without the hindrance of government intrusion. All indications were that by the middle of the nineteenth century this newfound freedom opened the door to widespread economic prosperity in England and its colonies. Englishmen at this time were better paid, better fed, better housed, and had more leisure than their counterparts in other countries.

It is perhaps interesting that in spite of the great economic success this freedom produced, there arose growing attacks on the social order and the policies that made these achievements possible. To be sure, the initial attacks were made by a small cadre of disgruntled social observers. Nevertheless, in time their criticisms gained ground and resulted in a wider variety of new attacks. The essence of these attacks centered on identifying ongoing social ills and pointing out the failure of economic freedom to resolve them. In this way the criticisms amounted to various combinations of abstract rationalism combined with liberal doses of romanticism. That is, the critic would appeal to an abstract ideal that has never existed in human history and then complain that freedom has failed to overcome the imperfections of this world. They would then make a sentimental appeal to the reader to embrace some kind of social reform.

Not all those who engaged in such criticism of capitalism were socialists, but all the attacks provided more than a little grist for the socialist mill. Socialism has an almost irresistible attraction to a certain turn of mind. It is attractive because its criticism and rejection of the way things are rings true in people's minds, and its promises of the way things will be when they have been reconstructed are desirable. Given the many dimensions of human failure in this world and the resulting damage done, it is easy to see the appeal of these arguments. The attraction seems very strong among intellectuals, especially those of a literary or artistic bent.

By the latter part of the nineteenth century, given the growing number of criticisms, the proponents of evolutionary socialism had dramatically grown in number. Perhaps the most well-known of the socialist organizations formed in England during this time was the Fabian Society which was founded on January 4, 1884. The importance of this organization was not due to the size of its membership, but was more related to who its members were. It tended to attract men and women who were or would become leaders in a variety of intellectual fields. Among its members were George Bernard Shaw, Sidney and Beatrice Webb, R. H. Tawney, Bertrand Russell, Malcolm Muggeridge, and John Maynard Keynes.

The success of this organization in promoting gradualist policies in England lay in its strategy. Embedded in its efforts were continual calls for social reform. They made use of numerous other ideas and viewpoints around them to make their case. While the promotion of free enterprise sprung initially from a natural law argument, other proponents had argued for it based on Jeremy Bentham's utilitarianism. Unlike the natural law argument that all people possess the rights to life, liberty, and property, utilitarians argued that no such rights exist and that public laws should be based upon whether or not they increase the general welfare. While most utilitarians, such as John Stuart Mill, advocated for free markets, the Fabians found such a philosophy useful in pushing for social reform and widening the scope of socialist policies. Thus, they would identify some supposed failure of free enterprise and advocate governmental intervention as the best means of rectifying the situation. Indeed, such arguments tended to proliferate throughout the early part of the twentieth century in England. The high water mark for such socialism in England came after the Labour Party's sweeping election of 1945. The Labourites proceeded to nationalize all sorts of industries and to press its socialist policies in every direction.

Socialism in England failed miserably. The effect of such policies is to turn the power of government upon the nation's own people, thus depriving them of the ability to accomplish their productive endeavors. The government generally regulated, restricted, taxed, and confiscated the property of its people keeping them from producing the goods and services that were once widely available. The more that the government tried to redistribute property, the less of it that was available to redistribute. The result was nothing more than spreading hardship and greater poverty. Socialism cannot succeed. Its failure is inherent to its nature and cannot be separated from it.

In the 1980s, the failure of socialism did result in a political walking back from it when Margaret Thatcher became prime minister in 1979. This was a position she held until 1990. As the leader of the Conservative Party in England she set about to undo as much of the socialist agenda as was politically possible at the time. She lowered tax rates, privatized industries, opposed union demands, and stabilized the currency. As a result greater prosperity returned. This is not to say that the degree of free enterprise that the English once enjoyed was restored. Nevertheless, there was relatively more freedom. Following Thatcher's tenure in office the Labour party returned to power. Though they have not been as aggressive as previously, there remains a bit of a tug-of-war between defenders of freedom and those continually promoting evolutionary socialism.

Today the circumstances in the United States are pretty much the same as those in England. The main difference has to do with the kind of policies that brought the country to this place. Political cycles have moved in waves toward and away from socialism. Just the same, the general trend over the last one hundred and fifty years has been toward an ever-increasing number of rules, regulations, and restrictions on the American citizen. In recent years there has been a heavy push toward socialism though, like England, the U.S. experienced a retrenchment of such policies during the tenure of President Ronald Reagan. His two terms as president coincided with that of Margaret Thatcher in England. Perhaps the main difference between the socialist path in England and that in the U.S. has to do with the obstacles that the reformers had to overcome.

The change came slowly in the United States. As a nation, the United States has long been considered a bastion of freedom and opportunity. Immigrants poured into America from other lands in increasing numbers searching for better lives. They came, at least in part, looking for greater opportunity than what they had in the places they came from. For the most part they were not disappointed. That fact is owed primarily to the underlying principles on which the nation was founded. The American Founders were largely agreed upon a natural law conception of life in this world. That is, they agreed that the individual person had the right to his life, liberty, and property and that it was government's role to protect these rights. As a result, they established a limited constitutional republic assigned with the duty of providing such protection.

Americans were thus free to engage in productive enterprises as they saw fit according to their various skills and talents. No one was guaranteed success, but the Constitution stood as a mighty bulwark against those seeking to take one's property by political means. Government was thus strictly limited and this served as the biggest obstacle to the social reformers. The result was economic prosperity. This is not to say that the nation always held to its principles. In fact, there were some glaring inconsistencies. Perhaps the most obvious one was the continued practice of legalized slavery. After all, if a man cannot own his own labor and sell it on terms agreeable to him, what can he own? This kind of inconsistency threatened the social order.

Another contradiction of principle that threatened the social order was the continual effort of some to use the powers of government for special privilege. Alexander Hamilton for one was an advocate of imposing protectionist tariffs on imported goods. His justification for this policy was that he thought it would promote the growth of domestic businesses. However, such a policy is not in the general interest but rather benefits the favored few whose businesses enjoy reduced competition. Nevertheless consumers are harmed. The problem here is that government power is thus used to limit the choices of consumers making them hostages to certain business interests. This clearly violates the very foundations of personal freedom and liberty.

With the election of Abraham Lincoln in 1860, the two issues of slavery and protectionist tariffs came to a head. Lincoln's political lineage can be traced back to Hamilton. This follows since the Republican Party at that time carried the torch for corporatism that he advocated. Having gained political power the Republicans set about passing laws to promote private business interests. These included the Morrill Tariff Acts, the Pacific Railroad Acts, and other pieces of legislation providing special privileges to certain business interests. Apart from the rising tide of corporatism, the issue of slavery also came to the fore as well. This was an obvious factor. The combination of the two resulted in the Civil War.

As the saying goes, winners write the history books. Southern democrats had been firmly against the corporatism of Lincoln and the Republicans. But since they had withdrawn from the Union, and then lost the war, a new age more favorably disposed to granting special privilege began to emerge. As the utopian idea spread among American intellectuals of the day, the increasing corporatism provided an opportunity to press for more socialistic policies. The proponents of social reform called themselves Progressives and increasingly sought to take over both political parties.

Their success in doing so is most profoundly marked by the election of Woodrow Wilson to the office of president in 1912. From this point forward, America has been on a general path toward socialism with only a few setbacks along the way. Some of the key figures in promoting socialist policies include Franklin Roosevelt, John Kennedy, Lyndon Johnson, Richard Nixon, Jimmy Carter, both George Bushes, Bill Clinton, and most recently Barrack Obama. Under the guise of social reform and the promotion of the general welfare the nation has succumbed to the adoption of progressive income taxation for the purpose of redistributing wealth, the monopolization of money and banking by the creation of the Federal Reserve System, the regulation of business enterprise through a vast web of federal bureaus and agencies that restrict behavior in countless ways, and the increasing takeover of the nation's educational institutions.

While the problems created by corporatism are legion, and an uncountable list of examples could be given, there has been an ever-increasing size of the federal government. Its expenditures and taxes continue to escalate. In addition it has established a massive web of rules and regulations restricting the free actions of the citizenry. At this point it should be pointed out that all evolutionary socialistic efforts push nations relentlessly away from freedom and toward despotism. They result in a halfway house of sorts. While revolutionary socialism is always brutal, tyrannical, destructive, dictatorial, and dark, gradualism places nations in the twilight. Conditions in them are not as dark as they could be if total socialism prevailed. As a result, there is a tendency for proponents to argue that the existing light, however weak it may be, proves that their socialism is working. Nevertheless, all socialists are ideological brothers under the skin whether they be communists, fascists, Nazis, or gradualists. Moreover, if gradualists had their way in everything they wanted to do, they would take a nation to the same total darkness of the revolutionaries.

With this in mind we will briefly consider the case of Sweden, which is often pointed to by gradualists as proof that socialism works. The idea that Sweden is an example of working socialism first appeared in Marguis Childs' 1936 book, *Sweden: The Middle Way*. He argued that their socialistic policies were leading to major improvements in life in that country. However, Sweden, just like the United States and Great Britain, has an economy that lies somewhere along a spectrum from free enterprise to command and control. So the real question when examining whether socialism is working or not is, which parts of such an economy are reasonably well-functioning and why?

Long before Sweden embarked down the gradualist path to socialism, it participated in the great economic liberalization of free enterprise in the nineteenth century. As a result, it had enjoyed rapid economic expansion and engaged in a healthy amount of international trade with other countries. The result was the creation of a great deal of wealth for the people of that country. In addition, Sweden had the good fortune of avoiding many of the calamities of destruction that plagued other European countries during the two world wars. Thus, prior to embracing any socialism, its economy was strong.

It was only in the midst of this prosperity that Sweden ventured down the gradualist path to socialism, as did so many other Western nations. In the same way that these policies wreaked havoc on the economies of England and the United States, they are also hindering the economy of Sweden. It only appears that socialism in Sweden works because its socialist policies have not entirely overtaken private enterprise. That is, despite the high tax rates imposed on the Swedish population that fund its welfare state, businesses for the most part are still privately owned and operated for profits. Thus the benefits of private enterprise tend to mask the devastating effects of socialism wherever it is imposed.

At the end of the day, in all such cases, it is the individual who feels the weight of the force of gradualism that is being imposed on him. Since social democrats use the ballot box as a means for furthering their agendas, the individual is left isolated unless he can connect politically with some group. Even then socialists tend to press for greater and greater government intervention invariably asserting the need for some sort of intervention to correct some societal ill. Few ever ask whether such intervention is warranted. As such, government intrusion into the lives of people grows and if the individual will not yield to the weight of numbers, he is likely to be punished by the state. His only line of defense is his private property, which is increasingly infringed upon by the advances of gradualism.

Six

People Confused and Abused by Rules Gone Wild

Those who claim that everything must be regulated are correct. However, that fact should not be taken to assume that government should be the regulating agent of all things. Prices of goods and services are regulated in a free market by supply and demand. The potential for profits tends to increase the supply of things, which in turn tends to keep prices low. Better quality goods and services sell for higher prices and poorer quality at lower prices. When demand for an item increases its price goes up. This leads some to seek for alternatives and tends to attract more producers of similar goods. In short, the principles of economics are at work regulating our interpersonal affairs.

The market, as the late Ludwig von Mises was fond of pointing out, is democratic in tendency. It responds to the most widespread and urgent demands. The market, as such, has no values, no standards, no morality, except such as are fed into it by buyers and sellers. If buyers and sellers are devoid of ethics, then the market can be a dangerous place full of cheats and thieves and fraught with peril for would-be participants. But, such a complete moral breakdown is more likely to result in the breakdown of free enterprise altogether. Free enterprise requires private property and that requires a moral respect for those rights. If morality is breaking down it is not likely that such property rights will be respected. Moreover, the easiest way for one group of people to abuse the rights of another is to use the power of government.

The market may be value free, but society is value laden because people are by nature valuing creatures. We all have a sense of right and wrong. Moreover, we all have our individual desires and ends: our tastes and preferences. Our interaction with one another and our shared values are the things giving rise to society and the market is a mechanism by which we interact economically. Society is the normal regulator of the market, bringing standards, values, taste, judgment, ethics, and morality to bear on what takes place there. The economy works best in a civil society that has high standards of conduct.

A free society regulates the market through its approval or disapproval of acts. Public decorum, ethics, morality, and civility are maintained because the individual seeks the approval of the other people around him as well as the approval of God. It seems natural to many of us to wish to be in good standing with those whom we come in contact. One seeks the good will of his employer for many reasons, not the least of which is to keep a job. Children obey parents out of love and respect and because their livelihood depends on them. People behave themselves not only because they wish to be well thought of but also because their well-being in general depends upon it. When these financial and familial supports are cut away, social directives lose their bite.

Increasingly today government has assumed much of the role of the family. Compulsory school attendance and government guidelines of what must be taught relieves parents of much of their responsibility for their children and authority over their upbringing. Welfare and Social Security payments chip away at the family by eroding dependence upon one another. The tendency of government intervention has been to minimize the family unit by removing much of its authority and responsibility.

The authority of employers has been drastically reduced as well. Every government mandate of wages, or working hours, or required employee benefits, has the effect of reducing the authority of the employer. As the authority of the employer is reduced and replaced by government oversight, the resulting impact on the workplace and the conduct of employees is sadly predictable.

A spirit of litigation afflicts Americans today. Patients sue physicians, students sue teachers, debtors sue creditors (we even have websites that offer advice as to how to do this), employees sue employers, wives sue husbands, and even children sue parents. What this signifies is the breakdown of society, the substitution of force for persuasion, and the intrusion of government into every nook and cranny of life. Those who bring suits may not realize it, but every suit invites the force of government to bring the parties into line. While a healthy tort system is crucial to a well-functioning economy, the rising tide of government rules and regulations leading to an ever expanding environment of aggressive litigation is not.

Whatever happened to the deal made between two people on the basis of a handshake? The social and cultural norms that bind us together as a society are being broken down, and with it trust and integrity are being replaced by rules, regulations, lawyers, and government force. But why is it happening?

There is an alien force in our midst. It is a pervasive influence that is foreign to our manners, customs, traditions, morality, and institutions. We are all familiar with it in one of its most obtrusive forms, that of the television or newspaper reporter. We have all seen such reporters, crowding around some beleaguered individual and badgering him about an offhand remark uttered in private that is secretly recorded and becomes the focus of an all-out media assault. Journalists crowd the person, pushing for attention, shoving microphones in his face and insistently demanding answers to questions that are none of their business. They are like wolves, baying at some prey they have surrounded, preparing to strip his garments away and render him helpless before them. They unsuccessfully try to maintain a professional demeanor, but cannot fully hide their giddiness as they mercilessly pester the victim of their onslaught.

Reporters, however, are only the most colorful of a much more extensive alien element. It holds sway on television and radio programs, and in the print and internet industries. It is often referred to as the media. However, in its broader dimensions it embraces much more: the entertainment industry, the fashion industry, the education industry, and a vast assortment of other businesses that lie on the periphery of these. In terms of its thrust, it should be called the "Transformation Industry."

Socialists regard the received social arrangements as a major detriment to their undertakings. Revolutionaries require that they be destroyed. Evolutionary socialists attempt to change them gradually by law so as to merge government with society. Revolutionary and evolutionary socialists both believe that the whole complex of distinctions that society maintains must be broken down before man can be collectivized. The received institutions, customs, mores and traditions that support and facilitate the smooth working of a free market must be destroyed before man can be melded into a mass.

With a few exceptions, the "Transformation Industry" is busily engaged tearing down traditional social customs and mores. And once decency is eliminated man can no longer be allowed to be free. Liberty for a corrupt man amounts to opening the gate and turning the beast out to forage at will. Such a man is no more worthy of property than would be a jackal.

The "Transformation Industry" is bent toward collectivizing us. It is stripping away from us our civility, our decorum, our good manners, our taboos, our traditions, and our individuality. Man must be reduced to be collectivized. His traditional values must be altered, or altogether eliminated.

The transformation of society that has been going on in the United States and around the world in gradualist nations proceeds by reversing normality. In effect, new norms are created, and the old norms are abandoned. This change is fundamentally necessary for proponents of the idea that has the world in its grip. They must turn normality on its head. They need to make what is normal seem exceptional and unusual. For example, there has been an aggressive effort recently to make it seem that hard work, prudence, and thrift are not normal and that no one could achieve financial independence by practicing these virtues. Instead, a vision that all people are more or less economic victims of an impersonal system called capitalism is the reason for personal financial failure.

The process by which this transformation occurs should be familiar for the pattern has been established by constant repetition and expansive application into more and more areas. The change is advanced by relativistic arguments. In the bluntest formulation the argument goes like this. What is normal? Who can say what is normal? At the ordinary level of discourse these are unanswerable questions. They are difficult to answer in the first place because we are not prepared to defend our concepts of normality. While we may be convinced that we know what normal is, giving proof that it is normal is quite another matter.

There is a good reason for this. Inquisitive children usually learn fairly early in life that questioning the norms is a fruitless undertaking. Far from being praised for their curiosity they are more likely to be maligned. After all, what kinds of questions can be raised about norms? Why do we walk on our feet instead of our hands? Why do we drive on the right side of the road instead of the left? Why do men have hair on their chests? Why do women have babies? In most cases no satisfactory answer can be given. Hence, children are discouraged from asking such questions. Moreover, the answer they've most likely heard before is, "That's just the way it is."

There is yet another reason for our inability to adequately defend our norms. One of the primary concerns of society is the maintenance of the norms. All social function depends on the general acceptance of a set of norms. Take them away, abandon them, and society disintegrates. Human action begins to lose its meaning. When the normal fades everything becomes unexpected and strange. To debate the validity of norms is to debate the validity and value of society. Civil society's business is to discover, preserve, and maintain norms that help promote peace and harmony in human relationships. Society's business is not to challenge the norms.

This is not to say that norms are not well grounded. On the contrary, the best norms are always those grounded in the nature of things. Where this is not the case because of custom, they were instilled by nurture. Either way, they serve an important function in our social existence. Their reason for being, if there be no other reason, is the smooth functioning of society. It is instinctually sound to resist discarding our norms. Not only that, but if we probe the matter deeply enough we may well discover reasons for our norms that we did not even suspect.

None of this is acceptable to socialists. The received norms always stand as a barrier to the socialist path whether that path is of the revolutionary or evolutionary variety. Socialism requires that all efforts be focused on achieving paradise on earth by coercive means. This is accomplished by first tearing down the prevailing social norms. The irony is that the goal of achieving utopia on earth by governmental means is now so widely accepted that it is itself a social norm—one that the socialists do not seem eager to attack. To socialists, acceptable norms become whatever is considered useful in controlling the individual and in politicizing society. Norms become those that are decreed by those possessing political power.

Socialists are concerned with breaking down the distinctions on which norms are based. This breakdown proceeds along two lines of attack. One is intellectual and its mode of attack is relativism. Relativism is used to discredit the accepted norms. According to this view norms are simply a matter of opinion or preference. As such, the authority for them is either a matter of majority opinion or that which a large number of people happen to do. What is normal becomes a matter of averages or the lowest common denominator of behavior. The logic of this approach is that if all norms are relative there are no norms. There is only what happens to prevail at any moment.

Another line of attack is to pose continual challenges to the established norms. Journalism is particularly well suited to this undertaking. There is an old saying that if a dog bites a man that is not news, but if a man bites a dog that is news. Journalists have a tendency to focus their attention on the odd, strange, curious, different, or unusual. But when journalism becomes pervasive, as it has in America today, it becomes a continual assault on the norms. With our twenty-four hour-a-day news coverage, TV journalists investigate almost every odd and horrific event imaginable. They interview some of the strangest people they can find and those with the most radical agendas. The result is that the unusual comes to be seen as commonplace.

The current hot button topic of same-sex marriage provides us with a road map for how traditional norms can be overturned. In those states where same-sex marriage is prohibited, almost daily a television journalist will locate and interview a same-sex couple whose desire it is to be "married." The interviews are usually done with an articulate and well-dressed couple. We are told, either directly or indirectly, that the traditional definition of marriage is outmoded and that we need to change our conception about what a family is. Indeed, we are persuaded that the traditional family unit with a husband, wife, and children is just one among many options in life. Fictional television shows pitch in with the likes of Modern Family and Grey's Anatomy focusing on same-sex couples raising children. In the process traditional values are first questioned, and later derided.

Let us emphasize why it is that the assault on traditional norms is necessary for the spread of the idea that has the world in its grip: Traditional norms reinforce morality, ethics, and honesty—the very foundation necessary for people to thrive while being free to pursue their own self-interest. This must be wiped out if the idea is to prevail.

Religion is intertwined with self-interest in a number of important ways. The Christian religion bids the individual person to recognize his alienation from his Maker and to humble himself before his God so that he might partake in eternal rewards. The very offer of hope for salvation is made on an individual basis. One's response to this offer of salvation is then a self-interested act. Indeed, Marx believed that this religious hope was the undergirding support for capitalism and he rejected it outright.

On the surface, the socialist problem seems easy enough to solve. What is needed is to get people to abandon their pursuit of self-interest and devote themselves to the common good. Therefore, they attempt to isolate self-interest, to make it unacceptable, and something to be discarded. They think that such attacks will eventually get people to abandon self-interested behavior. But their solution is not that easy. Self-interest does not exist in isolation from all other norms. Instead, it is intertwined with the whole fabric of the received culture. Socialists have generally understood this, which is why they must undercut the whole fabric of normality itself.

Of course, many who are aiming to transform society are not purposefully pursuing any socialist agenda. They are simply trying to make money, so far as they are concerned. There is money to be made in pandering to man's baser desires, and there is nothing new about that behavior. However, it is not necessary for those under the influence of the idea to know it in order to be under its sway. There is a kind of demonic urge to the egalitarianism implicit in the idea that has the world in its grip. Women must be the same as men, all sexual orientations equal, and no lifestyle any better or higher than any other. Traditional norms might be fine for an old fogy, but the new enlightened folks are going to toss them aside and "lean forward."

To collectivize us all, private property must come under attack. The whole system of private property supports and rewards the pursuit of self-interest. The tradition that a person has a right to claim the fruits of his own labor places a premium on the pursuit of self-interest.

Moreover, the family is an enclave of self-interest as its members are bidden to look after the interests of the family as a primary object of human action. The institution of private property is so developed and bound to the interest of the family unit in the history of things that these must be destroyed if the socialist vision is to be realized.

The socialist's view is that the received norms of civilization are honeycombed with supports for and enticements to the individual to pursue his own self-interest. As they see the matter, the pursuit of self-interest is a norm because the whole fabric of society makes it appear to be so. In order to cut away the pursuit of self-interest, the whole structure of normality must be replaced. Those under the sway of the idea differ about the means to be used, and perhaps how drastic the surgery must be, but they basically agree over the problems presented by the received norms.

There have been several major thrusts of socialism in the United States. Until recently the most thoroughgoing of these occurred in 1930s with the Roosevelt administration. Roosevelt's New Deal brought into being a significant framework of governmental meddling in the economy that substantially altered concepts of normality and morality. Redistribution was the operative principle in many of the New Deal programs. From the establishment of the Social Security system to farm subsidy programs these policies all aimed to use the apparatus of government to take property from some people for the benefit of others. In addition, labor unions were given a privileged position whereby they could use coercion and force to get higher wages and better benefits.

Since the 1930s, the federal government has continued to expand into more and more areas of life. Government action has become ubiquitous in society as it involves itself to an ever greater degree in the economic affairs of the people. Everything from airports to the local police and schools to the provision of health care involves some kind of government handout, which entails greater control over life. The Federal hand is not only in every pocket, it is also extended in every direction as more and more people seek freebies from government.

To those under the influence of the idea, it is an accepted premise that one of the essential roles of government is to control and direct the economy. Toward that end the government seeks to direct it by its spending and taxing and by its control over the money supply. It routinely manipulates the economy through its use of these devices. It creates artificial economic expansions through easy credit policies that drive interest rates below what market rates would have been. These expansions routinely lead to an economic bust when it is realized that the capital accumulated under them are not economically viable. There may not be one person in a thousand that questions the validity of our government's activities in using fiscal and monetary policy to "stimulate" the economy. It has become a new norm in the process of the socialist transformation.

Every traditional norm is grist for the mill. It is not clear in general whether it matters which norms are overturned. Since all traditional norms support the established order of things they must all be overturned. As such, it hardly matters whether what is involved is sex, marriage, the family, the role and position of the husband, education, limits on the authority of the President or government in general, ownership and control over property, or whatever. The attack on every norm weakens the authority of all norms, so any attack is useful. Still, priority is often given to those norms most deeply entrenched. It is from this angle that we can understand the assault on sexual norms in our society.

Sexual norms have long been established and would appear to be those that are most difficult to alter. Indeed, many sexual norms are rooted in nature. The general variations in the anatomy of men and women along with the differences and inequalities associated with them have been behind many of our sexual norms. Thus, it is reasonable to suppose that if these norms could be overturned a multitude of others would fall as well. Moreover, it should not be surprising that this is where much of the socialist attack has occurred, with the Transformation Industry leading the charge.

The reversal of the norms has a devastating impact on society. Norms are to society what the fixed points of a compass are to navigation. It can be argued that norms are relative, that some are even arbitrary. Indeed, some may well be. In similar fashion it can be argued that the directions on a compass are relative and in some sense they are. But it is absolutely essential to agree upon and accept them lest our navigation charts be rendered useless. Without that agreement no definite course can be plotted to go from one place to another. Likewise, the functioning of society is equally dependent upon general agreement and acceptance of a set of norms. Norms are the foundation of privileges, positions and functions within a society. When they are overturned the result is chaos in relationships. Without norms a person can no longer be sure what function he is to perform or who has the right or authority to make any decision or perform any act.

All constructive activity depends upon each individual knowing what he is supposed to do. Every undertaking involving two or more people must have a final decision maker. Moreover, we could hardly survive in this world isolated from our fellow man. We are social creatures. Given these facts there are always necessary authority structures in life that need to be understood and accepted if we are to live in harmony. Norms define this structure of relationships for us. When the norms are overturned, constructive activity declines and debates and contests over authority ensue. Force tends to replace voluntary cooperation. As a result, the strongest or most determined assert arbitrary authority.

This is what is happening in the United States as well as other nations where the idea is succeeding. While many people still attempt to live in conjunction with traditional norms they are nevertheless challenged on many levels. In addition, whenever anyone takes a stand for traditional values he tends to be ridiculed as a bigot, or a homophobe, or at least as an old-fashioned fuddy-duddy. The media plays a particularly important role here, rewarding those who conform to the "new way of thinking" and punishing those who do not. CEOs cower before the lash of enraged journalists, resign their positions, and retire to obscurity.

As legitimate authority structures break down, dictatorial authority rushes in. This can be seen clearly in regards to property rights. Anymore what a man may legally do or not do with and on his property is in great doubt. When contemplating any use of his property, a prudent person must now call in all manner of experts to weigh in on whether or not the proposed action is lawful. The experts won't know either, but they might give the owner a sense of his odds of getting prosecuted. This has resulted from the proliferation of laws along with mountains of government rules and regulations created by agencies assigned with the duty of implementing the laws. This has led to a massive web of red tape. In addition, it has put armies of lawyers to work as the court system has been burdened with what seems to be an endless stream of civil suits. In turn, the outcome of these suits only adds to the overall complexity of the legal restrictions imposed on the individual. The final result is that debates and contests over who has the right and authority to do something supersede constructive activity.

All of this has left the American people confused and abused. They have been repeatedly confronted and affronted by scandalous behavior. While rules, regulations, and restrictions on behavior have escalated beyond imagination, the maintenance of decorum and civility in relationships has declined. Those trusted with authority often abuse it routinely and engage in some of the most debased practices imaginable. Today politicians routinely lie about all manner of things. Even when caught lying, they often do nothing more than lie again. This has left the average American bewildered. That the political elite can seemingly get away with this behavior has left the average man fraught with doubt. He does not know what country he lives in anymore. He does not know what is acceptable and how he should behave.

Interestingly, the American people have been largely preoccupied. They have increasingly occupied themselves with their own affairs. Many have simply closed their eyes to what is going on around them. It is understandable that they should. The disintegration of society means that the individual can no longer rely on support in bringing reproach upon those who flout the norms. They can no longer count on the traditional means that discredit abusers of others to do the needed job. This means that the individual had best look to his own protection and well-being. But it also means that force will be brought to bear in more and more areas of life. The breakdown in traditional values and authority is not a prelude to liberation; it is rather the precondition of the establishment of authority by force.

Today that force is increasingly the force of government imposed upon people in ever-greater ways. Government intrudes ever more deeply into our lives, in ways too numerous to recite here. In the United States the National Security Agency now reads our e-mails and records our telephone conversations. The government forces us to purchase health insurance along government mandated guidelines. If we want to hire an employee, the government tells us what wages we will pay and what benefit packages will be offered. There is the continual sacrificing of control over our own affairs to those holding the reins of political power.

Socialists would like to replace the individual's pursuit of self-interest with the pursuit of the common good. There is no evidence whatsoever that this has occurred. True, politicians and their spokesmen from the Transformation Industry drone on endlessly about the common good, but the only obvious development thus far in its pursuit has been the disintegration of society and the decay of civilized behavior. Since the common good as best as anyone can conceive of it is bound inevitably to civilized behavior, it should be obvious that the socialist effort has been a colossal failure. Like the Russians before us, Americans are quickly losing any confidence in their government. There remains a growing cynicism about political action of any sort. But despite the confusion, people generally have not grasped or believed in an effective alternative. And so the grip tightens.

Seven

The Real Victim

The thrust of the idea that has the world in its grip is to take away the independence of the individual. To do so is inherent in the idea itself. It is also inherent in the socialist way of looking at things. Recall that the idea that has the world in its grip aims to focus all human effort on promoting the so-called common good. The way to achieve this aim is to make the individual a cog in a vast machine. That is, each person must be made to fit into the whole of the collective as those who see themselves as the designers of the machine conceive it. To centrally plan and control all of human life the individual cannot be permitted to act on his own. Total coordination of the entirety of human activity means that individual independence can no longer exist.

The idea runs much deeper than this. In addition to eliminating independence, the aim is to root out even the penchant of the individual to pursue his own self-interest. At its base, it is a religious, or at least quasi-religious, aim. In the socialist view, man's original sin is the pursuit of his self-interest. It is, they think, the source of all human ills in this world.

There is in socialism an unstated premise. That premise can be elaborated this way. Man has potentialities for both good and evil. One of his potentialities for evil is for the pursuit of self-interest without regard to the common good. They believe that over time institutional arrangements such as protecting private property were devised which support and license the pursuit of self-interest. According to their theory then, these institutions deform man. Marx held that man would finally be freed when the individual no longer pursued his own good but rather the good of all. Once achieved, the harmony that would result would be a great release from the tension born of each person seeking his own good.

Despite this theory, all the efforts expended to eradicate man's pursuit of self-interest thus far have been futile. The greater the effort to erase it, the more determinedly have men pursued their own interest as they conceive it. There is abundant evidence that even in the harshest environments the pursuit of self-interest persists. Take for example the nature of human action in slave labor or concentration camps. Despite the cruelest punishments, the inhabitants of these facilities continued to pursue their own interest. When a man is bereft of all else—wealth, family, position, religion, and the amenities of society—he still has himself as long as any will remains in him.

Attempts to wring out man's penchant to pursue his self-interest cannot succeed. The denial of the right to pursue self-interest is the denial of the right to life. Our very survival hinges on a lively interest in self. From the most primitive savage to the most refined and civilized man this has been true. Nor could it be otherwise. Each individual needs to be aware of and take the necessary steps to avoid the dangers that threaten him. He must either see to his bodily needs or it must be done for him. He must be constantly wary of things around him that can harm him: fire which can burn him, water in which he may drown, high places from which he may fall, objects that may fall on him, and a thousand and one other dangers that are routinely present in daily life. He must be on the lookout for ways to provide for himself and be on guard lest his provisions are taken away from him.

None of this is meant to imply that the individual is always alone in his effort to survive. Ordinarily, he may have help from others and render assistance in return. Society is founded upon mutually beneficial exchange and aid. Nevertheless, we must affirm that the individual pursuit of self-interest is as deeply imbedded in his nature as the will to survive, and necessarily so. There is no need to suppose that it is man's only motive, or always the predominant one. Contrary to the socialist's notion that the opposite to the pursuit of self-interest is the pursuit of the common good is the fact that its opposite is actually the pursuit of self-destruction.

Socialism cannot succeed at eradicating the individual's pursuit of self-interest. At best it can only induce him to conceal it by making hypocritical claims about the motives behind his actions. Socialism does not do what it cannot do. It only does what it can. It does not root out self-interest. Instead, it reduces and places formidable obstacles in the way of individual independence. The pursuit of self-interest is in man's nature. In contrast, the independence of the individual is not a trait stemming from the nature of things. It is something that is acquired. The assault upon independence is the way that socialists aim to force the individual to become a cog in the societal wheel.

Socialists use two main devices to take away and undermine the individual's independence. They are *organization* and *numbers*. First, they use organizations to bring people to heel to the wishes of the authorities. The most basic of these is government, but they also use other organizations as well. In the Soviet Union the secret police was perhaps the most diabolical of the organizations. It was empowered by the rulers to use whatever means necessary to subjugate the populace. In gradualist nations socialists attempt to infiltrate all organizations to make them instruments of government power.

Consider the National Security Agency's collection of e-mails and telephone discussions taken from internet service providers and telecommunication companies as a contemporary example. Edward Snowden famously exposed a fiendish public-private partnership in the area of snooping on individuals. In the so-called interest of "national security" many private businesses readily kowtowed to government requests for recorded personal conversations.

Socialist organizations are not restricted to government agencies—large bureaucracies often develop socialist tendencies even in the absence of the threat of government force. Large organizations evolve in free markets as a consequence of economies of scale arising from mass production and specialization. That is, many more goods and services can be created, usually at a lower cost with better quality, when they are produced in large volumes. People voluntarily enter into agreements with others to combine effort in production so as to achieve more output than would be possible otherwise. This is well known, and in many industries it is natural for large scale businesses to develop as a consequence of the economic benefits.

However, such large-scale production must be managed and this introduces some degree of bureaucracy. Large bureaucracies, including those that arise in the context of voluntary trade between consenting individuals, often tend to discount the value of the individual in ways desired by socialists. The employee sees his individual identity eroded as he is increasingly called upon to mouth platitudes that are politically correct, but are devoid of any connection to reality. The person's ability to think and act as an individual becomes less important than his collegiality when working as a member of a team—never mind that the team may end up doing little more than meet, socialize, and send one another mindless drivel in the form of e-mails. It is the truth of this kind of experience that so many have had in the corporate environment that has led to the popularity of the comic strip *Dilbert*.

Socialists wish to exploit large corporations to further their own ends. They also use the power of government to create special political privileges that promote the prospects for large businesses over and against their smaller competitive counterparts. Small scale businesses and entrepreneurs find it harder and harder to engage in productive activities because of the increasing regulatory costs imposed on them by governing officials. In this way an increasing number of people are forced into jobs working for large companies which become ever more bureaucratic and less efficient economically.

Fortunately, private enterprises differ from government in one important respect—when a firm becomes too bureaucratic its costs balloon and it is eventually forced out of business. The costs associated with a growing bureaucracy ultimately offset the benefits derived from the division of labor and mass production. Moreover, when the market is left alone entrepreneurs have every interest in devising new means of production that compete with and undercut the established way of business enterprise. Fresh new businesses spring up unencumbered by the interminable meetings, diversity plans, and team-building exercises that often characterize their larger competitors. Focused on profits the new startups are able to outcompete their large, top-heavy rivals.

In addition to using large bureaucratic organizations, the second device that socialists use to undermine independence is to reduce the individual to a number. There is undoubtedly an egalitarian animus behind socialism. The matter cuts much deeper than may be generally thought. It entails a continual assault on individuality. Everything that distinguishes one individual from another, all differences in personality, any uniqueness, any peculiarity, any rough edge, anything that would hinder or disrupt the individual's subservience to being a cog in the wheel must be sublimated, subordinated, or obliterated. He must be denied so that he might properly serve his masters. To do this, the individual must be reduced to a number, not a number with which to calculate, but a meaningless number.

Ludwig von Mises criticized socialism by demonstrating that routine economic calculations, such as a firm's estimation of its cost of capital, would be impossible in it. This is a useful insight, but matters are even more telling than this. The idea that has the world in its grip tends to banish all calculation and, with it, all thought. It does so by denying that there is any importance to the individual. The individual is to be subjugated. In truth though, all calculations begin with the individual. Indeed, so does all thought. The attempt to make the collective into the only unit of significance renders calculation superfluous and impossible. Human thought, creativity, and ingenuity become a disruption to collectivism and, thus, cannot be tolerated. It is for this reason that government must control the education system and refocus its effort away from systematic thought to indoctrination. They simply cannot permit real discussion and debate.

At first blush one might be tempted to think that socialists respect and admire diversity. Indeed, they often voice strong support of corporate affirmative action plans, and are strident in their opposition to any form of "discrimination" in their various discourses on such matters. But on the most important type of diversity—that being the diversity of thought—socialists cannot abide any difference of opinion.

Socialism cannot reach the point of total collectivism. Nevertheless, socialists continue in their efforts to press towards this goal. The ultimate aim is to reduce the individual to a nullity. An individual is known by his name. That name has a magical quality to it. It has been said that the most pleasing sound to a person is his given name. There is good reason for this. A person's name stands for his personality, for his individuality, his uniqueness, his differences, and all he has become and done. He who loves and respects himself must in some fashion love his name. Religious ceremonies sometimes give public sanction to the sacramental quality of the name. For instance, in Christianity the naming of a child is often coupled with his baptism. This public display of naming the person confers upon him a special importance and value.

Numbers, too, have meaning. They have a culturally prescribed, fixed, and precise meaning. They are devices for calculation. They convey magnitude and are useful for keeping quantitative records. The size of a number is determined both by how many digits there are and in what order they appear. The zero is invaluable in calculation for with it numbers can be rounded off and extended indefinitely. However, if it is not preceded by some ordinal number it expresses nullity. It is nothing.

What does all of this have to do with the subjugation of the individual? It provides the framework for understanding how socialists attempt to reduce the individual to nothing symbolically. The reduction is real and the symbols are a way of seeing it.

The assigning of numbers to individual people has much greater significance than we ordinarily think. While the assigning of numbers may have some use for the purpose of identification, that is not its primary significance. Take for example the numbering of prisoners. The prisoner's number is the state's stamp of ownership. It is a sort of branding. A prisoner is stripped at the outset of much that sets him apart from other people. He loses his possessions, clothes, and standing in the community. He also loses many of his legal rights. The state's number is the seal of his new status.

Alexander Solzhenitsyn, with his special insight and sensitivity, has suggested more about the importance of assigning numbers to prisoners. Here is an abbreviation of his account regarding the assignment of numbers to prisoners in the Soviet Union during the Stalinist era:

> Then again, they quite blatantly borrowed from the Nazis a practice which had proved valuable to them—the substitution of a number for the prisoner's name, his 'I,' his human individuality, so that the difference between one man and another was a digit more or less in an otherwise identical row of figures.... Warders were ordered to address prisoners by their numbers only, and ignore and forget their names. It would have been pretty unpleasant if they could have kept it up—but they couldn't.... In work rolls, too, it was the rule to write

> numbers before names. Why before and not instead of names? They were afraid to give up names altogether! However you look at it, a name is a reliable handle, a man is pegged to his name forever, whereas a number is blown away at a puff. If only the numbers were branded or picked out on the man himself, that would be something! But they never got around to it.[29]

Numbering people is a means of dehumanizing them. Most of us probably never think about it, but naming something fosters an attachment to it. The act of naming something or someone attributes personality. Anyone growing up on a farm can likely attest to the animals that you would name and those that you would not name. You would probably name the milk cows and horses, but never the pigs since they were being raised for their meat. To name such an animal would have made it much more difficult to kill and butcher it. To name it would have distinguished it from the others as if it were a pet.

Numbers are often essential for the purpose of legal identification of mass produced items. Thousands of automobiles are produced which are, for all practical purposes, nearly identical. Ownership of any particular vehicle is typically claimed by a title stating the automobile's VIN (vehicle identification number). The VIN is the differentiating mark that allows the owner to lay claim to it. However, there is a great difference between applying a number to a manufactured thing and to a person. When a number is applied to an individual, far from adding to his distinguishing features, it tends to make him much more like everyone else.

In America numbers were first assigned to people in the armed forces. While numbers on a "dog tag" may be useful for the identification of someone in a time where modern warfare can leave little else by which a fallen soldier may accurately be identified, that is not likely the whole reason for them. Indeed, the military works best when the individual is fitted into its organization. The military seeks uniformity, obedience, and conformity. The soldier in the army is made to be a cog in the wheel. Whenever a lone soldier might be encountered during battle, he would most likely be asked what unit he belonged to rather than asked his name.

The majority of Americans were first assigned numbers in the 1930s when the federal government established Social Security. Under the terms of the legislation the assigned number was made mandatory for employment. The whole government system marked a shift in ownership and control away from the individual to the government, but the designers of the system held that this was necessary in order to track the individual's "contributions" to the Social Security "fund." In truth, the money confiscated from employees no longer belongs to them. The individual no longer has any claim on the funds except as he might qualify based on the government's specified criteria.

Since its inception the individual's Social Security number has been used in numerous ways, including serving as a taxpayer identification number. Through the federal income tax the government is able to assert control over all of an individual's income since Congress decides how much of it to take according to their changing rules of income taxation. The individual is left to protect himself as best he can in an effort to keep what he believes is his amid these ever changing rules.

Moreover, the government attempts to manipulate the rules in order to direct the individual's choices in certain directions. Thus, some sorts of behavior are encouraged while others are discouraged. The government directs behaviors to encourage those things that are deemed to be beneficial for the collective, thereby tightening the idea's grip. As an example, consider the tax breaks that were available in 2014 for purchasing all-electric cars. If you purchased a car that runs on fossil fuels you had to pay more in taxes. However, if you purchased the societal "approved" electric car then you paid less. In this way—by increasing or reducing your family's standard of living—you are pushed to and fro. (Grumble about it to those under the sway of the idea and you will be chastised that you should quit your complaining and be happy that you live in a "free country" where you get to vote for your officials.)

Taxation is just the tip of the iceberg when it comes to labeling an individual by his or her social security number. All sorts of businesses in a variety of ways now use the social security number. When you open a new bank account you are asked to provide it. When you call the phone company to change the terms of your cell phone plan you are asked to provide your number's last four digits, and so on and so forth. Paradoxically, at the same time your number is being used for more and more purposes you are advised to carefully guard it so as to avoid the growing problem of identity theft. While the problem of identity theft cannot be entirely blamed on the use of social security numbers, it is certainly a major contributing factor.

This assignment of numbers to people is essential to those who aim to promote the idea that has the world in its grip. Identifying numbers are an attempt to reduce the individual to a level that he may be adequately dealt with by employing the least amount of effort. It reduces him to a few keystrokes on the laptop. Demoting the human being to a number often brings with it numerous complications as a person grapples with the various bureaucracies that he encounters. If someone else uses his identity—his social security number—he will have to spend countless hours and resources settling the problem. There are many who claim that these problems can be solved by more government oversight and regulation. This is an appeal for an ever-greater government role in the economy, trying to remedy problems that were largely created by the government in the first place. More regulation in such a situation would be like pouring water on a drowning man.

Socialists speak eloquently about their love for humanity, yet their actions toward individual human beings betray that declaration. In practice they tend to have real problems with actual people. To be sure, there are always people in our lives that rub us the wrong way and it takes more than a little of the grace of God for us to live with them. This is why the socialists often speak of "the people" in an abstract way. "The people" are lovely and loved. However, concrete individual human beings are loathsome. The solution is to reduce the individual to an abstraction. Fit him into an organization and reduce him to a number. If he persists in emerging as a full-scale individual human being, punish him by whatever means are available until he sees the light.

The government's assigning of numbers is not only an assault on an individual's personality, but also on his property. Naming something implies that the thing being named is either owned or possessed by or entrusted to the person doing the naming. For example, when a family acquires a pet they are likely to name it. It becomes the family's dog. When a rancher brands cattle he is pronouncing ownership. Likewise, assigning a number to something asserts a claim on it. As such, it is a subtle device that can readily be used to declare that what was yours is now mine or under my control. Again, consider the assigned Social Security number, which is used as the taxpayer identification number. Using this number in this way is a governmental grab for power. It is an assertion that government is the potential possessor of all property and income. Should you resist the government's grab of your property the final result is the government's use of force to cast you into a barred cage.

In the revolutionary form of communism the individual's property is abruptly taken once for all. It is accomplished by violence in an immediate fashion where the individual is given the choice of relinquishing everything or being shot. In the evolutionary form, the seizure of one's possessions occurs more slowly and gradually over time. In this form the individual is divested of his freedom and possessions step by step.

When in the grip of the idea false arguments are advanced to promote the notion that government must manage the affairs of the people in order to secure a better outcome than the one that exists at any moment in time. Whether it is controlling the money supply, transportation, health care, or education, statists relentlessly argue that government is best suited to the task. As a self-fulfilling prophecy of sorts, every time they succeed in pushing through more government control the individual is robbed more of his own economic wherewithal and his independence. As a result, he tends to give up and live as a ward of the state becoming less and less the human being that he was meant to be.

Reducing him to a statistic through the process of voting further facilitates the subjugation of the individual. The democratic process of evolutionary socialists turns voting into a kind of self-sacrificial act by which the individual gives up some of his independence to the elected official. By casting a ballot he turns over to government more of his independence and control of his own affairs. In turn, he is reduced to an anonymous number and becomes more a statistic. He is a scratch or mark on a ballot. Moreover, if the only choice on the ballot is between which method of subjugation he is most inclined to prefer, the whole process undercuts his individuality. This is increasingly likely in modern democratic nations. Anyone wishing to manage his own affairs is less likely to find any acceptable option on the ballot.

While voting for candidates may be a reasonably satisfactory method of determining *who* shall govern when government is restricted, it is hardly suited to determining *what* government should do. But this is where gradualism intrudes on the process. What government should do is a question that should only be answered constitutionally. That is, the limits of government should be clearly stated after consideration is made of the full value and weight of the individual man.

Socialism turns voting into a quest for the Holy Grail. It turns the mundane business of selecting who shall govern into the choosing of religious leaders who are assumed to be competent to manage the transformation of man and society. So long as a choice of candidates remains, voting is important, of course. It does restrain politicians to some extent to know that they will have to stand for election. Power can never be absolute so long as its exercise can be modified by decisions of the electorate. But for those who do not accept the religious vision of socialism, voting is a game of chance, with the odds arranged heavily against them. The path is inevitably in the direction of the consolidation of power into the hands of fewer and fewer people.

Power is never complete until it is arbitrary. Control over people is never as great as it might be until it is by whim as it came to be in North Korea under the Kims. So long as a reason has to be given for a particular action, power is somewhat restrained. If power is to be fully consolidated, then the individual must ultimately be made a zero so that he may be fitted into the organization of the power broker's choosing. Such power pushes us towards meaninglessness. It reduces human action to acts that have no discernable purpose for the individual. It is an interesting fact of modern life that it has only been in recent history that walls have been built to hold people in nations instead of keeping aggressors out. Why? Because people will flee from those exercising this kind of power over them if the pressure is too great. Given the chance to gain their individuality and freedom people will naturally pursue it.

Eight

Embracing Responsibility

> Freedom hath been hunted around the globe. Asia and Africa have long expelled her. Europe regards her like a stranger, and England hath given her warning to depart.
>
> — Thomas Paine, *Common Sense*[30]

A massive struggle is going on in the world. It is nothing less than the existential struggle for the survival of individuality. It is a covert struggle, ordinarily so well concealed that no report of it is made in the media. But it is a struggle that once understood becomes visible all around us. It is the struggle over who knows what is best for the individual's ultimate happiness, and who should be able to control the means by which it is achieved.

Those who are in the grip of the idea, who truly believe that maximum happiness on earth can be attained if we merely coordinate all of our efforts, will justify almost anything in order to attain their elusive end. Contemporary intellectuals believe that they are capable of rising above the rest of humanity to see what others supposedly cannot see. They essentially view man as nothing more than a sensual being caught in the grip of his own passions and desires. They tend to view him as little more than an animal struggling for survival. As such, they view mankind as a herd in desperate need of a leader who can define what should be the ultimate collectivist vision and motivate *or force* total compliance. They tend to reduce the individual to a social security number, a credit score, an NSA data point, or a node on the information superhighway. They believe that they, alone, are capable of determining the common good and imposing it upon the rest of humanity.

On the other side of the struggle are individuals who find ways to make their own choices, to control their property, and to retain their privacy and freedom in thought and action. They find ways to pursue their personal happiness in life for the benefit of themselves and those who matter most to them. Those who truly believe in the importance of individuality know that this world is going to be filled with its struggles and hardships. Some of these are the result of poor choices and some are the result of unfortunate circumstances. Whatever the case may be, they understand that surviving these struggles leads to growth and maturity; overcoming them builds character. While there are surely those in need of help along life's way, those on this side of the struggle know that the general condition of the individual should be one of freedom and liberty in the pursuit of one's happiness in this world.

J. Gresham Machen astutely understood this truth when he wrote:

> The whole development of modern society has tended mightily toward the limitation of the realm of freedom for the individual man.... It never seems to occur to modern legislatures that although 'welfare' is good, forced welfare may be bad. In other words, utilitarianism is being carried out to its logical conclusions; in the interests of physical well-being the great principles of liberty are being thrown ruthlessly to the winds. The result is an unparalleled impoverishment of human life. Personality can only be developed in the realm of individual choice. And that realm, in the modern state, is being slowly but steadily contracted.... When one considers what the public schools of America in many places already are—their materialism, their discouragement of any sustained intellectual effort, their encouragement of the dangerous pseudo-scientific fads of experimental psychology—one can only be appalled by the thought of a commonwealth in which there is no escape from such a soul-killing system.... The truth is that the materialistic paternalism of the present day, if allowed to go on unchecked, will rapidly make of

America one huge 'Main Street,' where spiritual adventure will be discouraged and democracy will be regarded as consisting in the reduction of all mankind to the proportions of the narrowest and least gifted of the citizens.[31]

Every year we pass through the various times and seasons. As spring approaches there are certain changes that we all come to expect and appreciate. In colder climates ice melts away and the weather turns milder. Spring rains water the earth and flowers begin to spring forth as do new leaves on trees. Birds can be heard chirping in the trees and the various colors of spring displace the gloom of winter. It is a recurring cycle.

Experience teaches that however hopeful and glad we are as spring arrives that we should also be wary as well. Spring typically does not arrive apart from great struggles in the atmosphere. Warm winds blowing up from the south collide time and again with cold winds from the north as winter grudgingly gives way to spring. This confluence of air masses gives rise to thunderstorms, heavy rains, high winds, even tornadoes that can all be devastatingly destructive.

But then on the heels of these storms there comes a special moment. It is a moment when the chill of the air gives way to the warmth of the sun. It's a moment when the brilliance of spring is on display and the fragrance of the blooming flowers fills the air. It is a time for a peaceful walk in the meadows or for sitting by a cool stream and reflecting on the blessings of life. In such moments we are probably as near to peace and harmony with nature as we are likely to get in this world. However, the world is not now in such a state of tranquility. Peaceful moments occur, but they are fleeting. Ever since the fall of man the world has been less than peaceful. It cannot be changed through the application of force any more than can collective action halt the arrival of a blizzard or change the climate. Nevertheless, collectivists somehow believe that they can achieve such peace and harmony by using force.

Despite all their efforts, people continually resist. Resisting the oppression brought by collectivism infects every walk of life and every sort of activity. When working in bureaucracies the resistance evinces itself as malingering, as carelessness, as unconcern, as extra trips to the water cooler, as inefficiency, and often as nothing short of sabotage at work. It is done by professors at universities who never teach but regularly assign "group projects" to students. While the students seem to be busy, they actually learn very little while making it easy on the teacher. People resisting the collective are quite imaginative as they individually seek their own betterment while evading the rules and regulations of the collective. Resistance occurs when income is concealed from government or when individuals attempt to cling to some of what is theirs by carefully sheltering their income, wealth, and property. Often, only the individual knows his means of resistance for he would be subject to penalties if it were identified. If resistance is identified, governments stand ready to use force to bring the individual back in line with the collective for the common good.

Under collectivism, force and coercion are used to accomplish the ends as those holding the political power of the moment have defined them. But man is not merely a number or a cog in a larger machine, and it is not the job of kings and leaders to discern what constitutes the highest social end and to impose it upon the individual from the top down. Early Christian writers were clear on the subject. In Book IV of *The City of God*, St. Augustine exposed the flawed logic in trying to justify government action that violates the natural rights of people:

> Justice removed, then, what are kingdoms but great bands of robbers? What are bands of robbers themselves but little kingdoms? The band itself is made up of men; it is governed by the authority of a ruler; it is bound together by a pact of association; and the loot is divided according to agreed law. If, by the constant addition of desperate men, this scourge grows to such a size that it acquires territory, establishes a seat of government, occupies cities and subjugates peoples, it assumes the name of kingdom more openly. For this name is now manifestly conferred upon it not by the removal of greed, but by the addition of impunity. It was a pertinent and true answer which was made to Alexander the Great by a pirate whom he had seized. When the king asked him what he meant by infesting the sea, the pirate defiantly replied: 'The same as you do when you infest the whole world; but because I do it with a little ship I am called a robber, and because you do it with a great fleet, you are an emperor.'[32]

Whether or not one agrees with our theism, it is unmistakable that the individual is responsible for his own life and should be free to exercise his own agency in the choices that he makes. Human beings are not merely the means to be employed by others to achieve their ends. Who would want to live in such a circumstance? The individual is of great value and ought not be forced or coerced to do someone else's pleasure.

Individual responsibility is the key that unlocks the door of the collective maze in which we are caught. There is no such thing as collective, organizational, or corporate responsibility. All responsibility is individual and personal. Men sometimes make such silly statements as if they are speaking for an organization. Of course this is impossible, for organizations have no thoughts that can be expressed. There is no collective guilt, for the collective has nothing with which to register guilt. Nor is there any collective responsibility.

Indeed, a fundamental flaw in collectives and organizations is their ingrained and irreversible *irresponsibility*. As soon as control is exerted over people—whether by private businesses or governments—they tend to believe they are no longer responsible for what they do. Make a complaint to someone in an organization and the most likely response will be: "Look, I just work here." Who has not heard it? What the person is saying is that he is not responsible for what the organization does. He knows that if he does not personally control what is being done then he is not responsible for it.

Likewise, individuals do not feel any sense of wrongdoing when they benefit from the actions of the collective that they know would be morally wrong if they did them themselves. As pointed out by Leonard Read:

> Now take note of a startling fact. Those who wouldn't personally steal a dollar from anyone will favor the government stealing for them [by way of taxation] and with no sense of sin or guilt.... 'I wouldn't steal your horse but it's all right if someone else does the stealing for me!'[33]

But trying to escape from our personal responsibility is not so easy. In one of his sermons Jesus addressed the matter of individual priorities, and in the process provided an important lesson in economics:

> And why are you worried about clothing? Observe how the lilies of the field grow; they do not toil nor do they spin, yet I say to you that not even Solomon in all his glory clothed himself like one of these. But if God so clothes the grass of the field, which is alive today and tomorrow is thrown into the furnace, will He not much more clothe you? You of little faith! Do not worry then, saying, 'What will we eat?' or 'What will we drink?' or 'What will we wear for clothing?'... But seek first His kingdom and His righteousness, and all these things will be added to you.[34]

Of course, this scripture should not be interpreted so literally as to suggest that an individual should not engage in productive activities. Nor are we to stop giving any thought to what we will eat, drink, or wear. If we were to do so, the cupboard would well be bare in short order. Rather, at least a part of the message can be stated this way: Do not engage in vain struggles to accomplish what cannot be done. (The immediate verse preceding this teaching reads, "And which of you by being anxious can add a single hour to his span of life?"). Thus, the real meaning of the teaching is that we should get ourselves in accord with the nature of things. We should let our efforts follow a natural course. If we follow the right path first, what is good and desirable will follow from our efforts. This is very practical advice.

In one sense this admonition provides an important principle of economic action that we all should heed. Anyone who is skilled at chopping wood will tell you that you should always split it with the grain. If you try to do it against the grain you will expend a great deal of energy without achieving good results. The point is that the best way is also the easiest way. It is the economic way. It suits us when we go about achieving our ends in the most efficient and economic manner. No one ever sets out to expend as much energy and effort as possible to achieve the least possible result. This goes against our very nature.

The idea that has the world in its grip is propelling us in what is profoundly the wrong direction. It has led to multiple disasters, and will continue to do so as long as we are under its sway. Proponents of the idea are fighting against the grain of human nature. It is an effort to transform man, to reduce him to those aspects thought to be "socially useful," to integrate him into massive systems, and to subjugate him.

In the effort the attempt is being made to use collective force to intimidate him. The goal is to transform society into an instrument of force. The effort aims to use government for ends for which it is neither suited nor effective.

All of this misdirected effort has produced a widespread and continuous struggle. In part the struggle is to determine who can possess and control property. More importantly, it is ultimately a struggle over who is going to control whom. Socialism in all its forms, whether it is corporatism, welfarism, fascism, or communism, aims to wrest the control of property from its rightful owner against his will and to give that control to someone else. Such control renders the individual impotent.

In the evolutionary socialism of Western democracies the seizing of control has come about through heavy confiscatory taxation and the establishment of an impenetrable web of regulations. Government subsidies and price supports that benefit the special interests of some are the means of robbery. Businessmen in gradualist countries generally use what leverage they have to influence government to provide special privileges that will enhance the value of their specific capital investments over and against the genuine property rights of other people. In recent years we have seen this come to the fore as some local governments have used the power of eminent domain to seize the homes of some people for the benefit of commercial developers. The justification for these acts was that they promoted the common good by generating a larger tax base. This is nothing short of legalized theft and it ought to be called that. Capitalism is often blamed as the cause of these privileges, but it is not. The real cause is the grip of the idea and its transformation of capitalism into corporatism.

People are not defective machines. While it is certainly true that selfish passions in the human heart have led to all manner of hardships for us, the answer is not collectivization. The individual is not someone to be reworked and fitted into some grand organization. He is a soul. He has both a mind and body and is meant to grow and flourish in the course of this life. Above all, he is meant to be responsible for himself.

According to the modern conception of mankind, the individual is at best forever a child incapable of managing his own affairs. The whole idea behind the modern welfare state in Western societies is that the individual is too imprudent to be trusted to care for himself. If left to his own devices they believe that the individual will run to ruin neither caring for himself nor planning for his future. Therefore, they assert, the government must do this for him. It must provide him with the education, housing, health care, and other needs of life. The modern state treats the person as if he is a perpetual child.

Richard Weaver captured this reality in his book, *Ideas Have Consequences*. He compared the situation to that of a spoiled child. As Weaver put the matter:

> The spoiled child has not been made to see the relationship between effort and reward. He wants things, but he regards payment as an imposition or as an expression of malice by those who withhold for it. His solution... is to abuse those who do not gratify him.... The truth is that he has never been brought to see what it is to be a man. That man is a product of discipline and of forging, that he really owes thanks for the pulling and tugging that enable him to grow.... This citizen is now the child of indulgent parents who pamper his appetites and inflate his egotism until he is unfitted for struggle of any kind.... [If he could realize the reality that something greater than himself exists, if he could recognize the virtue of God] and not simply respond to coercion—he might genuinely realize human progress.[35]

It is certainly true that we human beings are very imperfect, and all of us behave rather foolishly on occasions. We can all attest to the suffering we have caused others and ourselves by this behavior. However, the answer to our failures in this life is not to make us permanent dependents. Rather, the answer is that we need to grow up. We need to stand on our own two feet and accept personal responsibility. Our failure to accept responsibility has produced the void that has allowed force to rush in.

Today force is being universalized around the world. While that force has abated to some degree in some places where revolutionary socialism resulted in abject barbarism, it has grown steadily in the evolutionary variety. Gradualist socialism pushes us relentlessly in the direction of greater and greater government intrusion into our lives. This may well be of greater consequence than the barbarism of revolutionary socialism. It may yet turn out that gradualism results in something far worse than what occurred in the more isolated revolutionary experiments. Gradualist socialism prepares the way for the triumph of what may turn out to be a greater barbarism. By widely disseminating and embedding the correctness of the idea that we must coordinate all human action into prevailing popular opinion, it may well be that the stage will be set for much harsher treatment of individual people. Once the door has been opened, those who refuse to be "coordinated" may be subject to the most severe forms of punishment.

In this final chapter we are making an appeal to conscience. We are asking every decent person to consider soberly the current situation. There is not one among us with perfectly clean hands in today's spiraling decline of civilization. Whenever we have sought governmental solutions to our material problems we have called for the use of force and coercion to extract something from our fellow man for our own use. In doing so, we have participated in causing the decline. It does not matter what our intentions were. It does not matter whether the goods in question were education or health care or something else thought to be necessary for our own advancement of life. Anytime we advocate transfer payments from others we are calling for violence to be used against our neighbors to achieve our own desired ends. Governments simply have no ability to provide such things without violating someone among us.

Collectivism is grossly irresponsible and it promotes greater irresponsibility among people generally. While socialists outwardly claim that they are concerned about the needs of others, the claim does nothing more than conceal the reality of what is being done. In a collectivist environment every man grabs whatever he can, according to his position of power in the system. The lies of the politicians are of little value to the most downtrodden and oppressed among us. Their vain promises are nothing more than a filthy reminder of the concealed greed that is really at the heart of their plans.

In contrast to the decline of individual responsibility and personal liberty that we are experiencing, we could have so much more. It is not for the individual to coordinate economies or to direct the efforts of others. The great task before us is one of *disorganization*, the disorganization of education, the disorganization of health care, the disorganization of banking, and so on. This can be accomplished mainly by removing government privileges, subsidies, and operations from all constructive activities. Moreover, each individual accepting the fact that he is responsible for his own life and thus breaking free from governmental dependency can do this.

There is an "Invisible Hand" that will take care of this for free and responsible individuals. When the individual is managing his own affairs he will study to produce what others will most readily buy. In so doing, he will serve the interests of his neighbors and truly promote greater peace and harmony. Songs and books will be written, discoveries will be made, fields will be plowed, and new inventions will be created. One cannot know what different sorts of ways free and responsible men will devise to get things done. We only know that free men will choose to cut the wood with the grain rather than against it because it is the economic way. It is the right way.

Acknowledgements

We want to thank Nelson Nash who prompted us to consider writing this book. We also want to recognize Clarence B. Carson. Dr. Carson's original book provided a rich foundation of keen insights and timeless truths for us to work with. Recognition also goes to his two daughters, Evelyn Mallory and Melissa Bean who graciously allowed us to use their father's work as a base for this book. We hope that it honors their father in every way. We would like to thank Hugh Whelchel, Larry Reed, Caleb Cleveland, and Michael DeBow for offering helpful comments on an earlier draft of the manuscript. We thank Dwayne Cogdill for his excellent cover design, and Ina Gravitz for her expert work in indexing the book. We also want to thank Roy Carlisle whose experience and wisdom in book publishing provided us with expert advice and counsel on many issues. Finally, we want to thank Cathe Cleveland whose tireless work in editing and layout were indispensable. Even though many people contributed to this final product, any errors that remain are ours alone.

Notes

1. Hedrick Smith, *The Russians* (New York: Quadrangle, 1976), 9–10.
2. Karl Marx and Friedrich Engels, *The German Ideology* (New York: International Publishers, 1970), 94–5.
3. Bertram D. Wolfe, *Marxism*, (New York: Dial, 1965), 361.
4. Karl Marx and Friedrich Engels, *Selected Works* (New York: International Publishers, 1968), 204.
5. Ibid., 209.
6. Wolfe, *Marxism*, 369.
7. Quoted in Thomas Molnar, *The Decline of the Intellectual* (New York: Meridian, 1961), 90.
8. Karl Marx: *Economy, Class and Society*, ed. Z. A. Jordan (New York: Scribner's, 1971), 126–27.
9. Ibid., 299.
10. Ibid., 292.
11. Quoted in David McLellan, *Karl Marx: His Life and Thought* (New York: Harper & Row, 1973), 118.
12. Ibid., 119.
13. Marx, Economy, Class and Society, 292.
14. Ibid.,292.
15. Leopold Tyrmand, *Notebooks of a Dilettante* (New York: Macmillan, 1970), 85–87.
16. Transcript of Fed Chair Janet Yellen's June 18, 2014 press conference, p. 5. www.federalreserve.gov/mediacenter/files/FOMCpresconf20140618.pdf (accessed on October 2, 2014).

[17] Bureau of Labor Statistics website: http://data.bls.gov/timeseries/LNS14000000 (accessed on October 2, 2014).

[18] Bureau of Labor Statistics website: http://data.bls.gov/timeseries/LNS11300000 (accessed on October 2, 2014).

[19] See U.S. Department of Education website: http://studentaid.ed.gov/types/loans/federal-vs-private (accessed on October 2, 2014).

[20] See Bloomberg Business Week website: http://www.businessweek.com/articles/2014-08-19/the-psychological-damage-of-the-recession-is-not-going-away (accessed on October 2, 2014).

[21] Frédéric Bastiat, "The State," in *Selected Essays on Political Economy*, tran. Seymour Cain, ed George B. de Huszar (Irvington-on-Hudson: The Foundation for Economic Education, Inc., 1964), 144.

[22] David Granick, "Plant Managers and Their Overseers," in Joseph I. Nogee, *Man, State, and Society in the Soviet Union* (New York: Praeger, 1972), 198.

[23] Hedrick Smith, *The Russians* (New York: Quadrangle, 1976), 104.

[24] Leona and Jerrold Schechter, et. al., *An American Family in Moscow* (Boston: Little, Brown and Co., 1975), 104.

[25] Frédéric Bastiat, *The Law*, trans. Dean Russell (Irvington-on-Hudson: The Foundation for Economic Education, Inc., 1998), 12.

[26] Quoted in Edward H. Carr, *Socialism in One Country*, (New York: Macmillan, 1958), 31.

[27] Matthew 7:16a.

[28] Adolf Hitler, *Mein Kampf*, trans. Ralph Manheim (Boston: Houghton Mifflin, 1943), 577–78.

[29] *The Gulag Archipelago*, III (New York: Harper & Row, 1978), 58–60.

[30] Thomas Paine, *Common Sense* (Mineola, New York: Dover Publications, Inc., 1997), 33.

[31] J. Gresham Machen, *Christianity and Liberalism* (New York: The Macmillan Company, 1934), 10–15.

[32] Saint Augustine, Bishop of Hippo, *The City of God Against the Pagans*, trans. and ed. R.W. Dyson (Cambridge, UK: Cambridge University Press, 1998), 147–48.

[33] Leonard E. Read, *Notes from FEE* (March, 1979), 1.

[34] Matthew 6:28–31, 33.

[35] Richard M. Weaver, *Ideas Have Consequences* (Chicago: The University of Chicago Press, 1948), 113–15.

INDEX

acts of faith, 24
actuality
    absence of, in Soviet Union, 30–33
    Marxism and, 17–18, 24
alienation
    community and, 1
    of man from true nature by private property, 20
    Marxist promise of end of, 1, 21–22
    necessitates revolution, 20–21
    of worker from product of labor by capitalist, 20
anti-religious religion, Marxism as, 18–19
    self-interest as original sin, 81
    in Soviet Union, 51–52
    theft of property and, 43
Auschwitz, 50–61
authority structures, 78–79
    See also state

Bastiat, Frédéric, 41, 53
Bentham, Jeremy, 64
Bernstein, Eduard, 24, 62
Birkenau, 60
Bolsheviks, 54–56
boom and bust economic cycles, 77
bourgeoisie, overthrow of by proletariat, 21
bourgeois state, socialist participation in, 25
Brezhnev, Leonid, 57
bureaucracies
    as best managers of individual's affairs, 90
    efficiency and, 84
    government and private, undermine individual freedom, 7, 44, 83–84
    irresponsibility of, 97
    resistance to, 95–96

capital, 20, 22
capitalism
    versus corporatism, 99
    in England, 62–63, 64
Childs, Marquis, 67
Christianity
    individual salvation, 75
    naming ceremonies, 85–86
    Soviet failure to destroy, 51–52
City of God (St. Augustine), 96
class struggles, 22
Cobden, Richard, 62
collectivism
    importance of, 25
    irresponsibility of, 97, 101
    Nazi, 59

collectivism (cont.)
  negates individual freedom, 81
  organic unity as goal, 61
  projection of guilt and, 61
  requires elimination of distinctions, 72
  resistance to, 95-96
  as socialist goal, 85
  use of force and coercion, 96
commodities, value of, 18
common good
  civilized behavior and, 80
  evasion of paying for, 6
  intellectuals beliefs about, 93-94
  loss of liberty in pursuit of, 94
  as part of utopianism, 8
  socialism and
    pursuit of, leads to freedom, 82
    replacement of pursuit of self-interest with, 75, 80
Common Sense (Paine), 93
communism
  deceptions
    examples of, 31-33
    as necessary part of, 30-31
    reasons for, 33-35
  determination of correct ideology, 32
  fear as result of, 40, 41
  necessity of ideological success, 34
  political corruption in, 40
  terror and tyranny necessary in, 56-57
  See also socialism
Communist Manifesto, The (Marx and Engles), 16
community
  alienation and, 1
  coarseness in human relations, 50-51
  destruction of bonds of, 48-49
  entire, supports self-interest, 76
  government regulations bewilder, 78-79
  as regulator of free market, 70
  role of norms in, 73, 77-78
  voluntary organizations, 50
Conservative Party (England), 64
coordinated effort
  individuality disrupts, 9
  must be by government, 10
  as necessary to achieve utopianism and happiness, 9, 10, 26
  state as force behind, 10
  through socialism, 15
corporatism, 66, 67, 99
creativity, stifling of, 48
crime, 42-43
culture
  as cause of selfishness, 9
  delusion of necessity to remove, 45
  destruction of
    as necessary for emergence of social man, 21-22
    as necessary to achieve utopianism, 11-12
    as prelude to tyranny, 12-13
    relativistic arguments for, 72-73
    by revolution, 12
    will end self-interest, 45
  enables individual freedom/individuality, 10, 27, 45
  entire, supports self-interest, 76
  government as force to alter, 10
  role of norms in, 73
  value laden nature of, 70
cynicism, as result of deceptions, 39-40

Das Kapital (Marx and Engels), 16, 62
deceptions
  cynicism as result, 39-40
  do not have to be believed, 39
  media role, 36
  as necessary for socialism/communism, 30-31, 35
  property theft as not theft, 44
  purpose of, 39
  in Soviet Union
    for domestic and foreign consumption, 33-34
    government and constitution, 32-33
    government officials, 35
    industrial power, 41-42
    religion, 33
    use of statistics, 46

in US, 31
    interest rate management, 36-37
    labor market participation, 37-39
    privileges of leaders, 35-36
    use of statistics, 37
dehumanization and numbers, 87, 89
delusions
    ability to change human nature, 44-45, 46
    freedom with massive government, 44
    necessity to remove cultural supports, 45
    triumph of proletariat, 42
democracy
    free market as form of, 69
    socialism and
        evolutionary, 25, 90-91, 99
        impossible with, 34
        participation in bourgeois state, 25
        pretense of, 31, 32, 33
        revolutionary, 58, 60
        theft of property, 42
dependency, 11, 27, 41
dictatorial authority structures, 78-79
Dilbert (comic strip), 84
disorganization, importance of, 101-102
displaced persons (DPs), 3-4
displacement
    of culture, 11, 12-13
    degrees of, 4-5
    sense of place and, 4
    types of, 4-5
diversity, 85

economy
    boom and bust economic cycles, 77
    control by state
        central planning, 47, 48
        results in less productivity, 41-42
    development of large scale production, 83-84
    in England, 62-64
    manipulation of, by state regulations, 76-77
    mercantilist, 62
    productivity of property, 41-42, 44
    protectionist policies, 66

as result of human actions, 27
socialist dilemma, 44-45
as source of ills, 27
Soviet collapse
    by 1921, 55-56
    as cause of collapse of state, 42
    industrial power deception, 41-42
    NEP and, 57
successful requires creativity and innovation, 48
in Sweden, 67-68
tort system and, 71
in US
    interest rate management, 36-37
    labor market participation, 37-39
    public opinion about, 39
    role of debt, 38-39
    stagnation due to federal regulations, 48
See also free enterprise/market
education
    government intervention in, and erosion of family, 70
    religion and, 12
    in US, 38-39, 94
egalitarianism, 84-85
elections and socialism, 58-61, 62, 64, 90-91
employment, US Bureau of Labor Statistics definition of, 38
Engels, Friedrich, 16, 17, 20, 62
England
    as birthplace of evolutionary socialism, 62
    economy
        under capitalism, 62-63, 64
        under socialism, 64
equality and privileges for powerful, 33, 35-36
evolutionary socialism
    alienation and, 21
    compared to revolutionary socialism, 24-26, 67, 90, 100-101
    democracy and, 25, 90-91, 99
    England as birthplace of, 62
    as impossible due to alienation, 21
    intellectuals and, 23-24

evolutionary socialism (cont.)
   legally through ballot box, 58-61, 62, 64, 90-91
   main components of, 25-26
   as more recent tactic, 53-54
   private property seizure in, 90
   regulations as method of, 62
   relativistic arguments to change norms, 72-73
   in Sweden, 67-68
   tactics of, 26

Fabian Society, 63-64
family
   assault on
      by government, 49, 70
      labor productivity of women and, 55
   as enclave of self-interest, 76
   social norms and, 70
   as unnecessary for state, 55
fear, as result of communism/socialism, 40, 41, 56, 57-58
Federal Reserve (US), 36-37
figurative displacement, 4, 5
free enterprise/market
   community as regulator of, 70
   in England, 62-63
   large corporations in, 84
   regulation by, 69
   requirements of, 69
   in Sweden, 67-68

German Ideology, The (Marx), 15
Germany, 58-61, 86
Gorbachev, Mikhail, 58
government. *See* state
gradualism, 25
gradualist socialism. *See* evolutionary socialism

Hamilton, Alexander, 66
happiness
   achievement of
      requires coordinated effort, 10, 26
      requires totalitarianism, 11
   greatest, as crux of utopianism, 8-9
   individuality and, 9
Hindenburg, Paul von, 58
history and Marxism, 19, 22
Hitler, Adolf, 58-61
human interaction. *See* community
human nature
   importance of following, 98-99
   self-interest as part of, 9, 45
   socialist delusion that, can be changed, 44-45, 46
   utopianism and, 10
   and values, 70
human rights, basis of, 63-64
Hume, David, 62
hypocrisy of communism, 30-31

ideas, acceptance of, 3
Ideas Have Consequences (Weaver), 100
ideologue versus insane person, 42
independence, 11, 27, 41
individual freedom/individuality
   achievement of happiness and, 9
   alienation and, 20
   culture supports, 10, 27, 45
   delusion of, within massive state, 44
   under English Conservative government, 64
   global struggle for existence of, 93
   names and, 85-86
   numbers and, 86-89
   ones who pursue, 94
   regulations restrict, 67, 78-79
   responsibility for self and, 97-98
   rights of others and, 2
   socialism as destroyer of, 21-22, 27
      bureaucratization and loss of, 83-84
      inherent in nature of, 81
      reduction to nothing, 84-87
      by removing cultural supports, 41, 45
      by theft of property, 99
   state management of affairs as self-fulfilling prophecy, 90
   traditional norms support, 75
   uncritical acceptance of ideas and, 3

in US
    examples of government restriction of, 79, 83
    history, 2, 65
    utopianism and, 8-9
individual responsibility, 97-98, 99-100, 101-102
innovation, stifling of, 48
insanity, defined, 42
intellectuals
    appeal of Marxism to, 23-24
    in Fabian Society, 63
    use of relativism to change norms, 74
    view of individual, 93-94
interest rate management (in US), 36-37
interpersonal relationships. *See* community

Jews and National Socialism, 59, 60-61
journalism and establishment of new norms, 74

Khrushchev, Nikita, 57
Kollontai, Alexandra, 55

labor
    alienation of, 20
    government regulations and erosion of owners' authority, 70
    rights to fruits of own, 65, 75-76
    unions during New Deal, 76
labor market participation (in US), 37-39
labor theory of value (Marxism), 18, 22
Labour Party (England), 64
law
    relationship to state of, 56
    use of, by evolutionary socialism, 58-61, 62, 64, 90-91
Law, The (Bastiat), 53
Lenin, Vladimir, 54-55, 56
liberals, as evolutionary socialists in US, 26
Lincoln, Abraham, 66
literal displacement, described, 5
litigation in US, 70-71

Machen, J. Gresham, 94-95
macroeconomics, as pseudo-science, 46
Marx, Karl
    biographical information, 16-17, 62
    characteristics of, 16
    conditions for revolution, 55
    end of alienation, 1
    as father of all socialism, 16
    as intellectual scavenger, 19-20
    revolution as necessary to achieve new society, 15
    triumph of proletariat, 42
    See also revolutionary socialism
Marxism. *See* revolutionary socialism
media
    as agent of collectivism, 72
    assault on traditional norms and establishment of new by, 74, 77, 78
    described, 71
    as participants in spreading deceptions of powerful, 36
Mercantilism, 62
Mill, John Stuart, 64
Mises, Ludwig von, 69, 85
money supply, manipulation of, 76-77

names versus numbers, 85-87
National Security Agency (US), 79, 83
National Socialist German Workers' Party, 59
natural law, 63-64, 65, 96, 98
nature. *See* human nature
Nazi Germany, 58-61, 86
New Deal (US), 76, 88
New Economic Policy (NEP, 1921-1928), 57
Nicholas II (czar of Russia), 54, 55
norms
    authority structures and, 78-79
    end of traditional, and creation of new, 72-73, 76, 77, 78
    family and, 70
    purpose of, 71, 78
    role in community, 73, 77-78
    self-interest and breakdown of, 79

norms (cont.)
    self-interest's integration with other, 75
    socialism and, 73-74
    traditional, support individual freedom, 75
North Korea, 48, 91
nudity, 12
numbers
    as assault on private property, 89-90
    names versus, 85-87
nurture. *See* culture

Orthodox Christian Church (in Soviet Union), 33

Paine, Thomas, 93
past, sense of place and continuity with, 12
perfection, attainability of, 2
personal responsibility, 97-98, 99-100, 101-102
place, sense of, 4, 12
Politburo (Soviet), 32, 35
pragmatism of evolutionary socialists, 25
Presidium (Soviet), 31
private property
    abolition of, 21
    alienation of man from true nature and, 20
    family and, 76
    free enterprise and necessity of, 69
    government regulation of, 78-79
    numbers as assault on, 89-90
    ownership and achievement of potential of, 43
    ownership in Sweden, 68
    productivity and, 44
    pursuit of self-interest and, 75-76, 81
    theft of
        destroys individual freedom, 99
        Marxist, 42-44
        and redistribution of, 64, 67, 76, 88
        in revolutionary versus evolutionary socialism, 90
Progressives (US), 26, 66

proletariat
    delusion of triumph of, 42
    end of class struggle with victory of, 22
    overthrow of bourgeoisie by, 21
    See also workers
propaganda, effects of, 49
public nudity, 12

Read, Leonard, 97
Reagan, Ronald, 65
reality
    absence of, in Soviet Union, 30-33
    Marxism and, 17-18, 24
refugees, as displaced persons, 3-4
regulation(s)
    economic effects of state, 48, 62, 70, 76-77
        See also economic collapse *under* Soviet Union
    evasion of state, 5-7
    by free market, 69
    restrict individual freedom, 44, 67, 78-79
    as weapons of evolutionary socialism, 62, 99
    See also taxation
relativism and norms, 72-73, 74
religion
    alienates individual from self, 20
    intellectuals and, 24
    Marx and, 16
    Marxism and, 18-19, 24
    naming ceremonies, 85-86
    salvation and, 75
    severed from education, 12
    socialism as secular, 8
    social man requires destruction of, 31
    in Soviet Union, 33, 51-52, 55
    as subservient to state, 49
responsibility, 97-98, 99-100, 101-102
revolution
    alienation necessitates, 20-21
    displaces received culture, 12
    evolutionary socialists and, 25
    as necessary to achieve new society, 15

as necessary to steal all property, 42
as scientifically necessary, 22
tyranny as result, 22-23
revolutionary socialism
    achievement of, 54-55
    anti-religious religion of, 18-19
    appeal to intellectuals, 23-24
    compared to evolutionary socialism, 24-26, 67, 90, 100-101
    destruction as essential to, 22
    impossibility of success of, 34
    key concepts, 19
        labor theory of value, 18, 22
        theft of private property, 42-44
        See also alienation
    legally through ballot box, 58, 60
    Nazi Germany and, 58-61
    private property seizure in, 90
    reality and, 17-18
    as replacement for religion, 24
    self-interest in, 82
    socialism as watered-down version, 24
    as system of thought, 17
    task of history, 19
    tyranny as implicit in, 22-23
    withering away of state, 26
    See also Soviet Union
Roosevelt, Franklin D., 76
rules. *See* regulation(s)
Russia, 54-55

same-sex marriage, 74
Say, Jean Baptist, 62
Schechter, Leona, 51
self-interest/selfishness
    culture
        induces, 9
        limits, 45
        supports, 45, 76
    family's role in, 76
    government regulations and, 79
    maintained throughout communist control, 49
    need for force to counter, 10
    as part of human nature, 9, 45
    persistence of, 82-83
    private property and, 75-76, 81

    rights to fruits of own labor and, 75-76
    salvation as, 75
    socialism requires abandonment of, 75, 80, 81
    structure of normality must be replaced to end, 76
sense of place, 4, 12
"slipping through," 5-7
Smith, Adam, 62
Smith, Hedrick, 5
Snowden, Edward, 83
socialism
    as answer to problems with English capitalism, 63-64
    collectivist goal as impossibility, 85
    consistent impetus toward, 26
    as conspiracy, 34-35
    deceptions as necessary, 30-31, 34-35
    as destroyer of individual freedom, 21-22, 27
        bureaucratization and loss of, 83-84
        inherent in nature of, 81
        reduction to nothing, 84-87
        by removing cultural supports, 41, 45
        by theft of property, 99
    determination of correct ideology, 32
    economic dilemma of, 44-45
    end of alienation and, 1
    fear as result of, 40, 41
    forms of, 99
    labor market participation and, 37
    necessity of success of ideology, 34
    opposes human nature, 45
    participation in bourgeois state, 25
    political corruption in, 40
    promise of fairness, 26-27
    received norms as barrier, 73-74
    requires elimination of distinctions, 72
    self-interest and, 75, 76, 80, 81
    theft of all property, 42
    in US, 66-67, 76
        See also Social Security (US)

socialism (cont.)
  use of large corporations to further own ends, 84
  utopianism and, 7, 9, 15, 53
  as watered-down Marxism, 24
  See also communism; evolutionary socialism; revolutionary socialism
"social labour," 18
social relations. See community
Social Security (US)
  erosion of family with, 70
  identity theft and, 89
  reduction of individual to number, 88
  theft and redistribution of property by government, 76, 90
society. See community; culture
Solzhenitsyn, Alexander, 86-87
Soviet Union
  achievement of revolutionary socialism in, 54-55
  coarseness in human relations, 51
  collapse of, 58
  community destruction, 50
  constitutions, 32-33
  economic collapse
    by 1921, 55-56
    as cause of failure of state, 42
    central planning and, 47
    human initiative and, 46
    industrial power deception, 41-42
  equality in, 33
  government of
    actual functioning of, 32
    deception of members of, 35
    surveillance of citizens by, 50, 83
    terror as control mechanism, 40, 56-58, 83
    theoretical structure of, 31
  historical periods, 57
  individual reduction to number, 86-87
  productivity of land, 47
  religion in, 33, 52-53
  self-interest maintained, 49
  "slipping through" in, 5
  women in, 33, 55

St. Augustine, 96
Stalin, Joseph, 56, 57, 58-59
state
  ability to produce rightdoing, 46
  as best manager of individual's affairs, 90
  coercion by, 41, 96
  determining limits of, 91
  expansion of, 40, 41-44
  as force to alter culture and reach utopianism, 10
  individual freedom and, 2, 44, 83-84
  as instrument of class rule, 20
  law relationship to, 56
  legitimacy of rulers, 56
  manipulation of economy by, 76-77
  norms and, 73-74
  restraining, 91
  role in utilitarianism, 64
  special privileges given to large corporations, 84
  surveillance by, 50
  as thief, 43-44, 96
  use of, to achieve maximum happiness, 10, 26
  withering away of, 26, 56
  See also Soviet Union; United States
"State, The" (Bastiat), 41
statism and evolutionary socialism, 25-26
statistics and deception, 37, 46
supply and demand as regulators, 69
Supreme Soviet, 31, 32
survival and self-interest, 82
Sweden, 67-68
Sweden: The Middle Way (Childs), 67

taxation
  machinations to reduce, 6
  manipulation of behavior by, 88
  manipulation of economy by, 76-77
  theft of private property by, 76, 88
  as weapon of evolutionary socialism, 99
tax inversions, 6
terror, 40, 41, 56-58
Thatcher, Margaret, 64, 65

tort system and economy, 71
totalitarianism, 11, 12
"Transformation Industry," 71, 72, 77
"truth" (Marxism), 19
tyranny
    displacement of culture as prelude to, 12–13
    as implicit in Marxism, 22–23
    as necessary to communist state, 56–57

unemployment, US Bureau of Labor Statistics definition of, 38
United States
    assault on norms in, 77
    bureaucracy and judiciary replacement of elected branches, 7
    Constitutional limits on government, 65
    deceptions in, 31, 35–39
    economy
        contradictions in, 65–66
        corporatism, 66, 67
        interest rate management, 36–37
        labor market participation, 37–39
        public opinion about, 39
        role of debt, 38–39
        socialist path of, 65
        stagnation due to federal regulations, 48
    education in, 38–39, 94
    individual as number in, 87–89
    individual freedom, 2, 65, 67, 79, 83
    litigation in, 70–71
    other names for utopianism in, 7–8, 26, 66
    political corruption in, 40
    regulations
        erosion of authority of employers, 70
        erosion of family, 70
        evasion and manipulation of, 5–7
        litigation allows further, 71
        restriction of individual freedom by massive, 67, 79, 83
    socialism in, 66–67, 76
    See also Social Security (US)
    surveillance of citizens by, 50
    tactics of evolutionary socialists in, 26
utilitarianism, 64, 94
utopianism
    common good as part of, 8
    displacement of culture as necessary to achieve, 11–12
    government as force to arrive at, 10
    greatest happiness as crux of, 8–9
    independence and, 11
    other names for, 7–8, 26, 66
    as secular religion, 8
    self-interest and, 9
    socialism and, 7, 9, 15, 53
        evolutionary, 62–68
        revolutionary, 58–61
    See also Soviet Union

value, Marxist determination of, 18, 22
voluntary organizations, 50

War Communism (1918-1921), 57
Weaver, Richard, 100
Weimar Republic, 58
Wilson, Woodrow, 66
Wolfe, Bertram, D., 17
women, in Soviet Union, 33, 55
workers
    alienation of, 20
    government regulations and erosion of owners' authority, 70
    proletariat, 21, 22, 42
    right to fruits of own, 65, 75–76
    unions during New Deal, 76

Yellen, Janet, 36

About the Authors

The Late Clarence B. Carson (1925-2003) was a native of Alabama, a graduate of Auburn University, and held a Ph.D. from Vanderbilt. Dr. Carson served in the U.S. Army, taught in high school and college at both the graduate and undergraduate level, and in later years devoted himself to independent research, writing and lecturing. In addition to fifteen books, he authored more than 500 articles and reviews which have appeared in such publications as *Modern Age, The Freeman, Chronicles of Culture, The Review of the News, Texas Quarterly,* and *Colorado Quarterly.*

Paul A. Cleveland is a Professor of Economics and Finance at Birmingham-Southern College. He received his Ph.D. in Economics from Texas A&M University. His principal academic research is focused on the study of free enterprise and political economy. In particular, he is interested in examining the proper role of government in society and the problems created when it enacts policies beyond its appropriate boundaries. He is the author of two books: *Understanding the Modern Culture Wars* and *Unmasking the Sacred Lies* and the co-author of the third edition of *Basic Economics* with Clarence B. Carson. In addition, his articles have been published in numerous places including the *Journal of Private Enterprise,* the *Independent Review, The Journal of Markets & Morality, Religion and Liberty, Areopagus Journal, Mises Daily Articles,* and *The Freeman: Ideas on Liberty.* Beyond his writing, he has lectured on free enterprise in numerous places including universities in Lithuania, Poland, Ukraine, Peru, China, and Taiwan. Finally, he serves as an adjunct scholar for the Alabama Policy Institute, as a part time scholar for the Apologetics Resource Center, and as a Senior Research Fellow for the Institute for Faith, Work & Economics.

Dwayne Barney is professor emeritus of finance at Boise State University. His undergraduate degree was from Weber State College and his Ph.D. in economics was earned at Texas A&M University. During his 28-year career at Boise State University he taught courses in the areas of economics and finance and was the recipient of a variety of teaching awards and recognitions. Administrative positions he held at the university included a stint as Chairman of the Department of Marketing and Finance and a four-year term as the university's NCAA faculty athletic representative. He is the co-author with Brian McGrath of one book, *Capital as Money*. As a researcher he has published numerous articles in professional journals such as *The Journal of Risk and Insurance*, the *Journal of Applied Corporate Finance*, and the *Journal of Financial Research*.